To Joey

Joey Sozzi
25 Macidonia
S.F. Calif.
285 - 1559 94110

100 Yamong

The Complete
Beginner's Guide to
MOTORCYCLING

The Complete
Beginner's Guide to
MOTORCYCLING

BERNHARD A. ROTH

Doubleday & Company, Inc.   Garden City, New York   1974

ISBN: 0-385-06382-2 Trade
        0-385-03537-3 Prebound
Library of Congress Catalog Card Number 73–11719

Acknowledgment

Generous assistance has been given the author in preparing, authenticating, and illustrating *The Complete Beginner's Guide to Motorcycling*. It has been very necessary help, in view of the far-flung, rapidly developing nature of the cycle sport and industry today.

Therefore, the writer warmly recognizes gracious contributions made by: Thomas Hannum, motorcycle dealer and veteran race-rider of Media, Pennsylvania; James B. Potter, Jr., executive director, and members of the Motorcycle Industry Council, Inc., Washington, D.C.; Edward DeRienze, photographer member, Pennsylvania Outdoor Writers Association; and finally, those pleasant companions of many a dusty cycle trail whose riding spirit and experience stimulated this book, the author's family, Claire, Anita, Roger, Darlene, and Robin.

Contents

*The Complete
Beginner's Guide to*
MOTORCYCLING

Sample the Fun

One day in the future, when you've been a "throttle-twister" longer than you can remember, someone will ask, "How come you took up riding a motorcycle?"

Your mind will go blank. Then you'll begin recalling. . . . Sometime, way back, you began to take special notice of these strange, peppy machines, with their helmeted and begoggled operators.

You could see that bikes were surely different from the big, plushy passenger cars and mammoth truck/trailers in the line of traffic. Those gleaming, bright-trimmed two-wheelers had a graceful zip about them, and their riders always seemed happy and carefree. You began to feel an urge building up in you somewhere. The urge got stronger as you pored over cycle magazines and catalogs and took to haunting dealer showrooms.

You'd sprint a couple of blocks just to get a closer look at some bike you hadn't seen before, and pester its rider with questions as long as he'd hold still.

Then came an unforgettable moment as someone observed your fever and offered to take you for a ride. Here was a milestone, the real beginning of your motorcycle adventure. Away you went, alert to every new thrill: the feeling of swift flight, the air hissing past

A day's outing with motorcycle and picnic lunch is one of the easiest and most enjoyable events for the new owner to arrange. *Yamaha Photo.*

your helmet, the whirring of tires pressing against the pavement, and the engine growling a message of power felt in the seat of your pants. Right there, you made up your mind you wanted more.

Everyone needs a checkride to make a fair decision. This isn't always easy to arrange unless you have a rider-friend or parent equipped to check you out. A dealer may offer a demonstration hop if he feels you're serious about buying. By all means, do not get on the buddy seat with just anyone. There are certain characters who specialize in scaring first-time riders half to death with bursts of speed and other "cowboy" antics. Hitch your initial spin with someone you can trust, and preferably aboard one of the heavier bikes, for seating comfort and maximum safety.

At this very instant, you're cordially invited to fill the buddy seat on your author's machine. We'd like you to get the feel of our heavyweight touring model. It has a two-cylinder engine designed to move us along at highway speeds easily, with power to spare. That means we can pull out of any tight situation in a hurry, in spite of our full load.

All right, let's make it "you and I" as a team. You, as passenger, can help make the ride a good one by following a few simple rules:

1. Balance yourself comfortably in the saddle, and keep your feet on the pegs at all times—while in motion and also while temporarily halted, such as at a traffic light.

2. Do *not* try to help the operator balance the bike. Let him or her worry about that.

3. Please don't lean way out of vertical to gawk around at the scenery, etc. This makes it harder for the operator to maintain balance, and it can be dangerous. Instead, you should peek over the driver's shoulder; or look elsewhere simply by swiveling your head.

4. Do *not* hang onto the operator with a stranglehold. Most comfortable and practical is to place your hands, palms open with a light touch, a few inches below the operator's armpits. In a split second, you can really put the clamp on him, if need be.

All set to navigate? Let's go, just as soon as your sunglasses or goggles are securely in place and your jacket is zipped snug. We don't want to be snatching at things while in motion.

Now let me fire up the engine and hop into position. You swing aboard after me. Right. Feet on those pegs and we're set.

It'll be hard for us to talk without yelling. Let's assume we have a little intercom phone system running between your helmet and mine. (Some riders have actually done this.) I'll try to furnish a few pointers as we go along. They'll come in handy as you learn to solo a bike later on.

We're moving out of the driveway into the street. The speed limit is 25 mph through the residential area. That's second gear for us, so it's easy shifting (first to second, then back to first) while threading our way through the maze of stop signs. Stop well to the right side at intersections, to be clear of drivers who enter a street by shaving off the corner.

Going down a steep hill, still in second gear, I'll take my foot off the brake and let the engine hold us back. And I'll go slowly and at right angles across the trolley tracks, here, where I once saw a cyclist take a nasty spill.

On the highway at last, the sign says 50 mph, but the traffic looks crowded, and we can see two sets of traffic lights up there ahead. Let's put the bike in third and edge up to about 45, with plenty of daylight between us and the car we're following.

Following at a safe distance will keep you out of trouble. *G. Smith Photo.*

I see the light go red, off there in the distance. I let the bike wind down to an easy-stop pace, rather than race up to a screeching halt. This makes the drivers in back of us take it easy. That way, there's less chance that we cyclists will be made the filling of a bumper-to-bumper sandwich.

We're in the clear beyond the last light for many a mile. The limit is 60 mph, and that's where I peg the speedometer needle. Strange how many motorists go right on by us, giving us a long stretch of pavement to ourselves. That's the way I like it. We can quit breathing exhaust fumes and enjoy the scenery. Also, other drivers can now see us plainly on our small vehicle. If they know where we are, we're that much safer in the saddle.

The miles roll away beneath us. Blue sky passes overhead; so do the clouds, birds, and a couple of jetliners. On either side, the countryside is a tapestry of wooded slopes, grassy meadows, hedges, and winding streams. It's a great day to be alive, on the move, and buzzing along on a machine that gives us the entire heavens and the earth to look at, with no interference.

Tailgating is a big no-no for all cycle riders. *G. Smith Photo.*

In the buddy seat, you're welcome to be completely at ease, taking it all in. I'm enjoying it too, but as the pilot, I'm not letting my guard down. I'm X-raying every little pothole, bump, and object in the road—inclining this way and that, delicately, to make sure nothing tosses us.

Watch out for side-slipping on loose sand or gravel. *G. Smith Photo.*

We're catching up with a huge semivan, going uphill. Feel that strong turbulence of air in its wake as we get closer. I look in the rear-view mirror affixed to the left handlebar. Nothing shows. But I'll doublecheck with a quick backward glance out of the corner of my eye. Nothing. Okay, let's signal left and gun 'er way out in the passing lane, and way on beyond, before we tuck in ahead of the truck by a good fifty yards. We settle down to more miles of gracious living in motion under the bright blue sky.

What do you know, it's lunchtime. How about a stop at my favorite roadstand for a quick dog and a Coke? I raise my left hand pointing straight up for an unmistakable right turn-off signal; downshift a notch; and decelerate into the parking lot, doubly wary of a bunch of loose gravel on the hardtop at the lot entrance.

Note: I park the bike in a prominent corner of the area. Right where I can keep an eye on it from inside the drive-in. Positioned where nobody can fail to see it. Why the strategy? Because careless motorists often overlook bikes when they glance in their mirrors.

Give other drivers plenty of notice of your intention to turn or change lanes.
G. *Smith Photo*.

They crunch right over them. Also, unwatched cycles are an open invitation to tampering and other monkey business.

Give me your helmet and I'll lock it up with mine in my bike's safari case. In this fashion, we can lolligag over our dogs and Cokes, all relaxed and serene.

Onward we go, angling toward home as part of the one-hour loop I figured would give you a reasonable sample. Smell that air— it's fresh. Take in that 360-degree arc of the horizon—that's the cyclist's way of life. But don't ever go limp, because here comes the dog in our lives. Maybe you didn't know: Many dogs pick on motorcycles as particular projects for their "chase anything" instincts.

I know this fellow and just where he lives. I like dogs; but aboard the bike, we just don't mix. So I'm ready. Full tilt down his lawn he comes, yipping all the way. As I'd planned, I merely pour on the throttle and am a hundred feet out of reach before he reaches the roadside. He's outflanked and falls well behind. Dogs are part of your cycling education and so are game birds and animals such as deer, particularly in the boondocks after dark. Just keep them in mind; don't be taken by surprise, and you'll be okay.

Finally, we're tooling into the suburbs again, back to the grind of stoplights, traffic signs, and the side-street, stop-and-go routine. A final first-gear crawl and we're right back in the driveway where we started. I kill the engine. You hop off first, and I join you, unfastening our riding gear.

I'd like to compliment your performance as a passenger-rider. The proof of the pudding is that I hardly felt you were there. I sure hope you enjoyed your ride. That sparkle in your eye must mean something!

Looking Them Over

The needs and expressed desires of some eleven million riders today encourage motorcycle makers to offer the widest variety of stylish performers in all history. Visits to just three or four first-class cycle dealers will reveal nearly the entire spectrum of riding tastes—all the way from the boulevard to the mountain peaks. Suitable units are right there on the showroom floor.

The only bikes you can't usually "buy off the shelf," so to speak, are the ultraspecialized machines required for expert and professional competition. Yet, the number of custom-special shops packaging these models is on the increase as cycle sports grow in popularity.

One thrilling day when your pocketbook feels right, and all other systems say, "Go," you'll go shopping for keeps. The vast array of bikes for sale may dazzle and confuse you. You'll need some guidance to emerge with a unit answering all your wants as you best know them.

Look for a dealer willing to discuss your plans patiently, with no high-pressure salesmanship involved. He'll ask reasonable questions about your experience as an operator; the price range that fits you; and, particularly, the kind of riding you picture for yourself. Then he'll show you his offerings.

It takes a lot of looking around and asking questions before that big decision, the first motorcycle, can be reached. *Ed. De Rienze Photo.*

This means preliminary thinking on your part. Information beginning in the next paragraph will help get your brain cells working. There are many ways to classify motorcycles. However, the following rundown covers essential details:

LUXURY MODELS

Starting at the top of the price line, here are the giants of the cycle world. They're big in most features beyond mere size. Included are roomy carrying capacities for two riders, and luggage spaces that invite long-distance camping and travel.

Dimensions, springing, shock absorbers, ample wheels, and tires —all spell the utmost in a comfortable ride. Elegant is the word for color finishes, chrome, and styling that appeal to the eye.

These are real highway machines, with attractions rivaling "cream puff" automobiles. They weigh in excess of five hundred pounds, usually. Buyers in this class often insist on all the trimmings: safety bars, saddlebags, extra lights, radios, cigarette light-

The six-gallon tank capacity for BMW R 75/5 means many miles between gasoline stops. This feature plus an electric starter and a luxury ride makes the
750cc husky a tourist's pleasure. *Butler & Smith Photo.*

ers, tape decks, the works. Prices, new, are in the two-thousand-
to-three-thousand-dollar range. What else does one get for all that
loot? Fantastic reliability is a key answer. This can mean as much
as seventy-five thousand miles of untroubled cruising, with hardly a
single mechanical adjustment.

SUPERBIKES

In a sense, these are stripped-down luxury models. They're big
and touring-oriented, but they give away comfort and elegance
for maximum performance. Buyers are the type who would probably go for a big-name, snorting sports car in a four-wheeler.

Engines and transmissions are designed to pour on maximum
horsepower and getaway capabilities. Fancy accessories are dumped
to save weight. Extras found on these models are strictly func-
tional, such as added carburetors, special suspensions, and other
items that increase "quickness" of motion. These "movers" price

The full-dressed luxury of Harley-Davidson Electra-Glide gives the rider that "king of the road" feeling when all those horses start to gurgle at the flick of the electric starter button. *Ed. De Rienze Photo.*

out in the fifteen-hundred-to-two-thousand-dollar range. You'll find them weighing in the four-hundred-to-five-hundred-pound brackets.

SUPERLIGHTWEIGHTS

Moving down the cost scale a few notches, we come to a type of machine that fascinates many riders. Superlightweights are a relatively new breed. Their aim is roughly to jam the height of performance into a medium-small package. Engines and engine accessories, gearing, weight, balance, handling characteristics, and styling are all zeroed in to "make 'em fly"; or, at least, to give the illusion of flight.

At the riders' insistence, engineers sometimes succeed in nearly doubling horsepower above the norm to be expected from motors of comparable size. The effect is explosive and results in lesser reliability, which any dealer will freely admit.

The intent here is not to criticize, but to tell it like it is. Riders who prefer the superjobs (whether big or little) receive razor-fine tuning in high-strung machinery. They soon realize that these units demand rather constant adjusting—and that wear and tear take a fast toll. Operators had best be fair to good mechanics, or prepared to pay the freight. Superlightweights scale at three hundred to four hundred pounds. Present prices run close to a thousand dollars.

A MIXED BAG OF LIGHTWEIGHTS

In this category is a fabulous collection of machinery to match a broad span of rider whims, moods, needs, fancies, and limitations.

At the top of the line are bikes with muscle and beef approximating the superlightweights—but without their fire and finickiness. These lightweights will carry all your freight in good shape and stretch out sturdily across the long miles in satisfactory fashion.

Lighter models of this class serve well for shopping; home-to-school-and-work tripping; jaunting to the drive-in; or just sheer pleasure-hopping around the neighborhood.

In this group, also, is found the go-anywhere partner for nearly any junket you can think of. Here are units feathery enough to rack up on a bumper or toss into a station wagon, trunk, trailer, boat, airplane, or whatever.

Versatility, flexibility, and multipurposefulness are the outstanding qualities of the lightweight. Practically all adapt to myriad situations, be it a tranquil asphalt surface or wild slopes where mountain goats await. New, off-the-floor prices are attractive. Featherweights begin at about three hundred dollars. More muscular designs range close to eight hundred dollars. As with bikes

A notably lightweight superbike is Mach IV Kawasaki 750cc rating 74 hp at 6,800 rpm's. The 3-cylinder 2-stroke is piston-ported and moves the 422-pounder over ¼ mile in 12 seconds, topping at 126 mph. *Kawasaki Photo.*

in general, you pay more for added performance. Weights straddle between one hundred and three hundred pounds.

A BEGINNER'S BIKE?

There is no such thing, really. Yet, since "What to get for openers?" is often asked, it deserves a reasoned answer.

On the negative side, do *not* buy the cheapest, tiniest, no-name brand popsicle on the market. Example: If a two-hundred-dollar bike hangs idle forever for lack of a twenty-cent part, where's the saving?

On the positive, do business with a reliable dealer and acquire the best you can afford, to suit your riding prospects. A-No. 1 considerations are sufficient power and size for your comfort and safety. Example: If you're a big, heavy person, the bike simply *must* be adequate to your physique.

The modified styling of the Harley-Davidson Sportster illustrates the combination of top performance and the hint of elegance built into this class of motorcycle. *Harley-Davidson Photo.*

Next, analyze your riding aims: Do they trend from short hops to fields and forests to cross-country journeys? Will you start with one aim and quickly branch to others? Try to imagine where you'll be with your rubber-tired charger months ahead—not just during your training period.

Most riders develop fast. They want to expand their activities as they absorb experience. On this aspect, one of our Pennsylvania dealers recently gave us several excellent opinions: "There's good reason to learn on an adequate lightweight. The machine, the sure-to-come dents and nicks, aren't too expensive. But pretty soon, a guy or a girl is looking for new worlds to conquer. Trading up the ladder costs 'a dollar,' which is all right for me. But I'm inclined to advise them to buy performance that will carry them at least a little ways beyond the learner stage."

We asked him if absolute greenhorns ever began at the summit, with a superluxury chariot worth two or three thousand bucks. "Oh, yes," he said, "we've had a few like that. They did all right, too. But I'd have to say they were mature, or mature-minded people, with natural ability and well-founded confidence. Nothing wrong with their bank accounts, either!"

In the springtime of our cycling, most of us have to settle for less. But we can always eye the horizon for greater days ahead.

SIZE AND WEIGHT—AND YOU

Beginners sometimes feel they'll never dare trying to master a big, beasty-looking highway machine. Although it's usually a good idea to gain confidence and skills aboard a fairly modest mount, the heavyweights offer pleasant surprises.

The big jobs, by their very size, enable designers to install numerous features that make for easier and safer handling. Heavies generally have more effective devices to absorb road shock, bigger wheels and tires, and deeper cushioning in the saddle. Coupled with a longer wheelbase, the effect is to smooth out the jounces and hug the road more firmly than lightweights do.

Greater size, again, often permits more convenient placement of the control levers, switches, buttons, indicators, and what-have-you. There's no need to bunch these items in hard-to-sort clusters, as sometimes happens on the junior models. The sheer poundage of heavies scaling up to eight hundred pounds and more is indeed a little awesome. If one had to lift them clean off their treads frequently, there'd be many a second thought.

The point is, these dreadnaughts were meant to be ridden. No

The Hodaka 100 BT. A lightweight off-road competition machine designed in the United States but made in Japan. It features rugged single-cylinder, two-cycle engine; excellent clearance; knobby tires; and big rear sprocket for better "thrust." The Hodaka is a fine off-road performer, but also, like others in its class, it has lights for legal public road use. It weighs about two hundred pounds and sells for around $650. *Hodaka Photo.*

less than startling is their ease of riding, despite all that bulk and heftiness. One key reason is their low center of gravity. Having ample size to play with, engineers can drop the heaviest components to the maximum. The only limitation is the need for road clearance, the highest obstacle a bike can straddle without getting hung up.

At least one popular heavyweight has a center of gravity *below* the axle line. It's a cinch to maintain upright in stop-and-go traffic.

To sum it up, size and weight are important in terms of a bike's performance. They need not stand in the way of a rider's progress. With increasing skill and experience, you can take 'em all on—and choose what you want to match the particular kind of riding you enjoy most.

Parade of Motors

The motor (or engine) is the heart of your bike. Its steady, strong, healthy pulsing measures the lifespan of your mount—more than any other component. So the saying goes: Love that engine, learn something of its "innards" and functions, understand its needs, treat it as a vital *living* thing—which it virtually is.

. One of the most dazzling attractions for two-wheel fans is the vast variety in cycle engine types. Beyond that are infinite modifications of basic designs. No other vehicle offers as many choices in power plants. As to performance, motorcycle engines have often led in pioneering ideas that proved useful to automobile- and aircraft-makers. Even today, auto engineers voice respect for the impressive power and durability built into ordinary, production-line bikes. High regard for bike "mills" is based on unusually stiff demands these devices must satisfy to qualify for motorcycle use.

There are practical limits on how much heavy hardware can be hung on two wheels. Bike motor designers *have* to be ingenious. Their genius shines brightest in the amount of "work" they can squeeze out of relatively small, light motors.

A standard ratio of "one-horsepower-per-cubic-inch displacement," for instance, is a rule-of-thumb for internal combustion

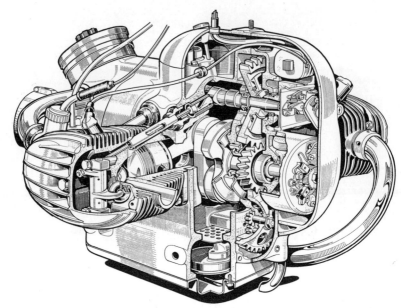

A cutaway diagram that illustrates the intricate workings of the BMW's highly successful horizontally opposed twin-cylinder four-stroke engine, which couples to a shaft drive, with autombile-style transmission. *BMW Photo.*

engines. (An exercise for your pencil: A cubic inch equals 16.5 cubic centimeters (cc). Thus a 300cc engine equals 18.1 cubic inches—and translates to 18.1 hp, according to the rule above.) Numerous cycle motors exceed that ratio in power output by a good margin. They grind it out steadily over thousands of rugged riding miles, with but minor care.

Year after year, cycle engineers step up their research, testing and trying, in pursuit of still better power plants. Constant improvement is the result. Meanwhile, experts are the first to declare: "There is no single engine that will do *all* things, to the satisfaction of *everybody*." Readers of this book will spend pleasant hours exploring the rainbow spectrum of engines powering today's models. Following are some indications of what's in store.

SORTING THEM OUT

Remember that there are two main kinds of "mills." One kind is called the two-cycle, also called the "two-stroke." The other

The vertical twin-cylinder-type engine powers many popular road and sports motorcycles. This is a 650cc Triumph vertical twin. *R. Roth Photo.*

kind is the four-cycle, or "four-stroke." Similar things happen in each kind of engine when running. Assume we're looking at two single-cylinder engines—one of each type. Each engine has a piston moving up and down, thus spinning a crankshaft, which (eventually) moves the bike.

In both kinds of engines, four definite actions occur. These actions are synchronized precisely with the movement of the piston: (1) intake of fuel-and-air mixture; (2) compression of fuel and air; (3) ignition (or firing) of the mix; and (4) exhaust (riddance) of waste gases.

A big difference between the two-cycle and the four-cycle in handling these actions is that the two-cycle mill fires *every time*

Kawasaki's 90cc Bushmaster engine has a rotary valve porting intake and exhaust system; this two-stroke has a separate oil-metering system for fuel mix. R. Roth Photo.

the piston approaches the top dead center (TDC) position; by contrast, the four-cycle fires *every other time* the piston approaches TDC. Another way to say it would be: the two-stroke fires once for *each* revolution of the crankshaft. The four-stroke fires once for *each two* revolutions.

Another sharp difference between the two engine types concerns lubrication—without which any engine would fast burn out. Lubrication oil reaches vital parts of a two-stroke engine in mixture with the gasoline vapor and air, either through the fuel line or a metering system. The oil is spewed about internally on important bearings and surfaces.

On the other hand, the four-stroke features a separate oil line, tank, oil pump, and oil-distributing mechanism. That is, the oil is conducted directly to engine bearings and other moving surfaces, and much of it is recovered for continuing use. Change of oil and

The overhead cam type of single-cylinder engine, one of the oldest, and still considered to be a very reliable four-cycle design. This is a Ducati Monza. R. Roth Photo.

replacement in a four-stroke can be compared to the needs of your family automobile, which is most likely a four-stroke.

A question may have arisen by now: Which is the better motorcycle engine, the two- or the four-stroke? This has to be answered with yet another question: *Better for what purpose?* Each kind of plant has its own pluses and minuses when applied to various jobs that bikes perform.

Give them all a workout, on the street, highway, or rugged trail. With experience, you discover the scarcity of *completely* true comparisons between the two breeds. Exceptions are many. Bear this in mind.

Basically, the two-stroke has a more simple design, in that it has only three moving parts: the piston, the connecting rod, and the crankshaft.

The four-stroke has these same moving parts, *plus* X number of other parts. These other mechanisms are used mainly to open and close valves that assist the intake, compress, fire, and exhaust phases described earlier.

In contrast, the two-stroke does not have mechanically moving valves, in the strictest sense. Intake and exhaust are handled via ports (holes) in the cylinder. These become open or closed as the piston or other moving part passes by the ports. There are minor variations of this principle. It's possible to build a two-stroke engine generally lighter and smaller than a four-stroke of similar displacement.

The two-stroke does not have valve-operating machinery or an elaborate oil-circulating system. Therefore, lighter weight metals may be used in the two-stroke engine casting; it doesn't need quite the strength to accommodate mechanisms peculiar to the four-stroke.

RIDERS' CHOICES

Study the two engine types for their special behavior patterns. Make your choice after a reasonable tryout. Here are typical experiences other riders have reported, in general terms.

Power delivery: Four-strokes usually furnish power more evenly over a broad "power curve," which relates to engine revolutions per minute.

Two-strokes tend to have a narrower power curve, usually concentrated in the higher RPM range. They may need added gearing. Where a four-stroke may do okay with a four-stage gearbox,

A big single-cylinder "stump puller" mounted in a BSA Victor proved a reliable four-stroker in hot competition ridden by England's famed Jeff Smith. *R. Roth Photo.*

a similar size two-stroke may want a five-stage gearbox. In this case the aim would be to use the extra gear to compensate for less power put out by the two-cycle at low RPMs.

Fuel and oil consumption: The better efficiency rating in using fuel goes generally to the four-stroke. Higher consumption by the two-stroke is roughly rated at 10 to 15 percent. However, the difference is in fractions of a penny per mile.

Ecology: Smoke commonly appears when a two-stroke first starts up. But burned oil itself is not considered poisonous; it just looks bad and, in excess, can be a nuisance. As to noise, two-strokes can scream, due to high RPMs. Yet, most engine sounds and emissions can be brought under reasonable control, as mentioned elsewhere in this book. This is true of two- and four-strokers alike.

Maintenance needs: The more complex gadgetry of a four-

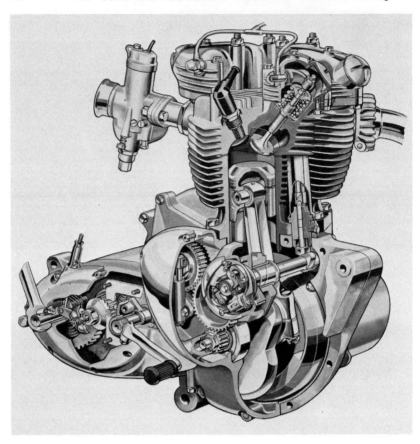

A section view of a 650cc Bonneville 120 engine. A vertical, twin-cylinder, four-cycle design. *Triumph Photo.*

cycle will require adjustment—particularly if ridden hard and long. A long, flat-out run for a two-stroke tends to be less troublesome, due to the fewer moving parts. Still, the latter will "coke up" (take on carbon residues) usually sooner than a four-stroke, and therefore call for more frequent spark plug changing and other defouling measures.

From the foregoing, you begin to get a "six of one, half a dozen of another" impression. The feeling grows as you roam through the dealer showrooms and examine the star-spangled array of power plants. Multicylindered "mills" in both categories . . . real "stump-pullers" of both kinds, including a three-cylinder two-stroke rated at 750cc . . . four-strokes with a dozen variations in valve arrangements . . . "hop up" kits for practically everything on the market.

These and other goodies will keep your engine happy indefinitely.

The Money Part

We doubt that anyone plunges into motorcycling *only* because it's a penny-saving sport. Yet the notable gentleness on the pocketbook has strong appeal. A fellow with the instincts of an Arabian sheik having a couple of oil fields to draw on may, of course, shoot a pretty good wad. A stable full of full-dressed luxury models, a few supers, and an assortment of dirt jobs will do the trick nicely. The average saddle fan can stretch his dollar to a remarkable length.

Facts about buying: Don't go "bargain hunting" for itself alone. A satisfying bike is always your main objective. Yet, dealers do have special sales. In the fall they may drop prices to clear the decks for new models, or just to close out their inventories. Cash in on this advantage when possible.

The quandary as to whether to buy used, or buy new, is likely to pop up. Elsewhere we touched on the merits of finding a reliable dealer. When you've done that, you buy more than just a bike: You buy his friendly interest and services as well. This fact can't be overstressed.

Buying used in a private sale depends . . . with a capital D. Are you mechanic enough to analyze the bike's shape? Can you get someone to do it for you? Will the machine pass state inspection? Is there a clear title of possession for it? Are you positive it isn't a

A young cycle enthusiast needs the advice and encouragement of an adult in the first selection of his motorcycle. *Ed. De Rienze Photo.*

stolen unit? Is the price right? Can you haul it to your house at reasonable expense? All questions should rate a straight yes, before going ahead. And, unless the machine's an orphan (no parts or service around), you may indeed save a fair amount of money.

Certain charges can't be avoided. They persist, whether purchasing through a classified ad or a dealer. To remind you that these realities do exist, here's a rundown on a new bike we recently bought:

Trail bike	$525.00
State sales tax (6%)	31.50
Insurance (125cc rate)	42.00
Registration & plate	8.00
Owner title certificate	2.00
Notary fee	2.00
TOTAL	$610.50

Had we bought on time payment, carrying charges would have added sixty to seventy dollars. In this connection, note that a buyer must be twenty-one or over to qualify for a mortgage on his own.

Costs of riding: For a true picture of cycle economics, you would also figure yearly depreciation in value; then add all the outlay on gas, oil, repairs, accessories—even incidental fun money spent on trips. Finally, you'd divide the whole business by your total mileage run.

This would be a gnat's eyebrow reckoning per mile. You'd reach one sure conclusion: The more you ride, the cheaper you ride, and the more adventures you'll have. Cyclists are cyclists, after all—not cost accountants. Most of us are content to know that our "weakness" doesn't knock the budget galley-west.

We'll rest on a couple of samples from our roving notebook. Here's one: "A thousand miles running around Nova Scotia on a lightweight for ten days . . . $6.75 for two-cycle-mix fuel." And another: "Six days of roaming the Outer Banks of North Carolina, 850 miles on a 600cc twin . . . $8.40 for regular gas and one quart of oil."

That's good enough.

A BIKE IS FOREVER

When buying a first machine, there's a tendency to go looking for a big deal, a bargain. The idea of saving a dollar or more is great. But don't get trapped.

The worst kind of trap is the bike that appears on the market with a big splash of advertising. Suddenly, a few months later, the ads vanish, and a few thousand riders hold bikes that no one (hardly) ever heard of.

A second-worst trap is a unit that never quite makes the scene. On arrival (like anything new) it causes quite a buzz. And it may be a pretty good wheel. But something happens: Manufacturers run out of promotion money; or dealers see little profit in it; or the bike appeals only to a limited number of specialized tastes. Outside of a limited area, the bike is a big unknown. Ask for help with it, and you're talking to yourself.

Reliable dealers insist that their salesmen discuss customer needs thoroughly and patiently, avoiding high-pressure tactics that might force a newcomer into an unwise purchase. *Ed. De Rienze Photo.*

Unless you're a mechanical genius, with your own machine shop facilities, take heed. Never buy other than a reasonably popular brand. Even then, be sure there's a dealer handy to take care of any problems.

There's a method you can use to check and doublecheck. Simply *assume* you've bought such-and-such a make and model. Now *assume* it needs some common service or ordinary part replacement. Call up the nearest dealer listed in the phone book. Ask him how soon he can fill your specified need.

Be guided by the response you get. First of all, is the dealer courteous and interested in your problem? Next, is the everyday part right on the dealer's shelf; or, if a specialized part, can the part be *assured* of delivery within a day or two? As to service, can the dealer *confirm scheduling* it quite soon?

Judge for yourself if the dealer gives a firm answer, or if he's playing games. Make allowance for the fact that bikes are a seasonal business over much of the United States; reliable shops *can* get jammed up, at the peak of the season. But a *responsible* shop-keeper will tell you the facts, tell you *exactly* where you stand.

From a number of inquiries, you can decide. Either your proposed machine is likely to receive good parts delivery and service—or it won't. On that basis, make up your own mind. And when the evening paper advertises a "Dodo Bird X-29½ in perf. cond. for $79.50, priced for quick sale"—think it over . . . and over . . . again.

You and the Law

All states now enforce laws that govern riders and their machines. A number of legal steps must be taken before *both* the bike and the operator can wheel freely down a public street.

Laws vary among states, and changes occur rapidly. The trend is toward making regulations the same everywhere. But watch out for states that don't have "reciprocity." You may get arrested for some technicality in a neighboring state, even though you're perfectly legal at home.

Even with unregistered bikes intended solely for use on private land, beware of booby traps. Some states frown on trucking or trailering such machines without a special permit. The moral is: Take a long look before you step into trouble.

Rider requirements: All states insist on a legal operator's permit. Qualifications, including minimum age, differ. For example, the state of Washington rules that motorcyclists must first take out a regular driver's license. A special endorsement is added to the license after the applicant has passed the cycling exam.

To get the endorsement, Washingtonians take a written general-information test of twenty-five questions. Passing that, they must demonstrate handling skills on a special course. Maneuvers include 180-degree turns, zigzagging around cone markers, and slow riding in a straight line.

Regular inspection by state authorities is a legal responsibility enforced throughout much of the United States. *Bernhard A. Roth Photo.*

Turn signals are required in some states. Designs that give the rider clear indication as to whether blinkers are operating or not are most desirable. *R. Roth Photo.*

Common causes of flunking road tests, throughout the nation, are "dabbing" a foot to the ground during a turn; failing to observe roadside directions, such as a stop sign; and neglecting to signal. A careless applicant may be denied taking the road test. Some have been rejected and penalized on the spot for showing up with an unregistered, uninspected bike—farfetched as it may seem. Others have been turned away for lack of a motorcycle-licensed companion on the day of the exam. Again, be sure to read the "fine print."

Remember that the laws affects you the instant you possess a bike. Part of your examination will include showing your owner's card and possibly a learner's ticket. Where compulsory insurance is in effect, you'll need proof you have it. Examiners will scrutinize you to insure you're wearing a helmet and goggles (or have a windshield) where these rules exist.

Motorcycle standards: "Street legal" describes a bike approved for public riding. To pass inspection, horn and lights—headlights, taillight, and stoplight—must be in good working order. Newer laws in some states also prescribe minimum wheelbase, wheel, and saddle height, in an effort to keep the minibike situation in hand.

As mentioned elsewhere, you can expect more rigid controls of sound and air pollution. Exhaust systems will be closely checked for noise and fume production. Some localities discourage altering motorcycles in any way. Outlawed are such items as "chopped" fenders and tailpipes, and extended forks. Common targets for lawmakers are so-called "ape-hanger" handlebars, having risers fifteen inches or so above saddle height.

Compulsory rear-view mirrors and turn-signal indicators are on the books here and there, as well as reflectors for nighttime visibility. If you carry a passenger, be sure your bike has both a passenger seat and extra foot pegs. Don't forget that helmet laws also dictate that passengers wear them.

Insurance: Even where insurance isn't compulsory, there are very few situations in which you can afford to skip it. A hundred-dollar premium is, for instance, a bargain, should you need to fight a hundred-thousand-dollar lawsuit or pay a judgment against you.

Agents will advise on the kind of policy you ought to have. If you're buying a bike in installments, the dealer will likely arrange insurance and specify coverage you *must* have. On application, your record will be checked as to accidents, law violations, and credit rating. However, you will *not* be charged extra premiums if you're under age twenty-five, as with automobile insurance.

Young or old, motorcyclists are treated alike.

Insurance costs are adjusted to the hazards of the area in which the bike is operated. Congested cities usually charge high premiums. Rates dwindle for suburban riders, and dwindle more for those based in remote, rural areas. A minimum policy, usually advised, will at least pay for average judgments that may be brought against you. Insurers call this "liability" for property damage and bodily injury.

In states that don't have compulsory insurance, it's smart to buy protection against uninsured motorists. In an accident, you may collect for damage to *your* property and injury to *your* person, if the other fellow can't make good, even if he's at fault. Should you carry passengers regularly, consider medical liability to pay for any potential injury.

From there on, it's a question of how much added insurance makes sense. When the cost of "comprehensive" coverage for fire, theft, collision, etc., begins to equal the value of the bike, you've doubtless reached the vanishing point.

The size of the bike governs premium costs. Most expensive are rates for the larger, highway models. The common scale used is based on engine displacement expressed in cubic centimeters (cc). Rates for a 250cc machine could be as much as 50 percent cheaper than for a 500cc policy. Only a half dozen companies insure two-wheelers in the United States. Some of these are controlled by the motorcycle industry.

Due to the seasonal nature of biking in many areas and other factors, motorcycle claims offices tend to be widely scattered. Prepare for this possibility. Carry your nearest agent's address and telephone number. Call him immediately in case of a problem, giving all the details. An adjuster will be around to see you, al-

Clear outlines of a full-scale motorcycle in reduced form are seen in this spirited minicycle fabricated by Steen's and ridden by a California youngster. *Steen's Photo.*

though perhaps not as fast as with an automobile case. We know of no instance wherein motorcycle insurers failed to back up their clients.

THE MINI'S A MYSTERY

Trying to define a typical minibike or minicycle is like trying to lasso a rainbow. That's what many state motor vehicle authorities are finding. Their problem is to rule on what kinds of minimachinery can be licensed for the road.

Permissible standards of performance for brakes, lights, horns, etc., are fairly easy to describe. The hard part involves suitable

The Suzuki TS-50J Gaucho has a two-stroke rotary valve engine and weighs 156 pounds. *Suzuki Photo.*

sizes and dimensions, including frames, wheels, wheelbases, saddles and saddle height, and horsepower. This is because minis are a vast assortment: wheels of 6-to-15-inch diameter; engines of 1 to 14 horsepower; speeds of 10 to more than 50 miles per hour; weights from 50 to 150 pounds.

That's only a beginning. Delaware, one of the first states to draw up mini regulations, specifies: 10-inch wheel rim diameter; 40-inch wheelbase; 45cc engine; 25-inch saddle. Any machine that can't meet any one of those *minimums* can't be registered for use on Delaware's public roads. Other states are making similar decisions. Be sure to check yours.

Saddle-up Time

If you can ride a pedal-propelled bicycle, you've learned the basic skills of balancing and steering a motorcycle. In fact, you should master a pedal bike first, to adjust more quickly. Handling an automobile does very little to prepare you for motorcycling techniques, except for a better understanding of traffic problems.

You'll need at least minimum physical strength in "manhandling" the motorcycle, holding it upright, and wheeling into take-off position. Once in motion, the powered two-wheeler is far more steady and solid in its tracking than a pedaled version.

Changes in direction for a moving motorcycle are made by the rider's *leaning* toward the desired turn and *following* the turn, to the needed degree, by angling his handlebars. This is exactly the same method as in normal bicycling.

For your early lessons, let's use a fairly large, open area. I prefer that we have solid earth or turf rather than pavement. This will prevent scratching the machine or yourself in case you happen to keel over. True, we may have to settle for whatever space is free.

First, I'll check you for safe riding attire. Stout shoes for your feet. Helmet and sport glasses or goggles for your head and eyes. Gloves for your hands. Substantial jacket and pants to save your skin. Nothing loose or flapping, to snag on the bike, or get in your way.

Getting off to a balanced start, a basic skill that the new rider must learn. *Montesa Photo.*

Together, we'll check the motorcycle. Plenty of gas in the tank, so that we won't have any surprise endings. Front fork unlocked and free-turning. Nothing clogging the wheels. Tires properly inflated. Drive chain has the right tension. Twist-grip throttle, clutch and brake levers seem all right. Horn, running lights, and brake lights okay. Shift lever normal and in neutral. Jiffy stand ready to be retracted. No loose nuts or bolts. No unusual leaking of gas or oil. We're all set.

An empty parking lot and an experienced rider to check your form will help your progress at the beginning. *Bernhard A. Roth Photo.*

Meanwhile, you've learned where the controls are located, and something else: The place to discover trouble is right in your own backyard—not somewhere out in the boondocks!

Now, swing a leg over—and take your time. Can you reach all controls handily? Kick the jiffy stand up and try coasting with *no engine power.* Use the foot-operated rear brake for leisurely stopping. Use both the hand-lever-operated front brake and the rear brake, together, for emergency stops. With a little shove from me,

Sturdy shoes or specially designed boots are recommended for better operation of foot controls and the prevention of mashed toes. *G. Smith Photo.*

let's see you balance and steer a reasonably straight course, both feet up on the pegs. Halt on a dime. See how long you can balance, motionless, without dabbing a foot. Great practice for slow-moving traffic that you're bound to encounter.

Whether your bike has a push-button or kick starter, the preliminaries to firing up the engine are the same. The gear shift must be in the neutral position. The gas must be turned on. Switch on the ignition. If the engine is cold, you may also apply choke. This provides a little extra starting fuel. From here on, experience will teach you your machine's peculiar little "firing up" habits.

Electric starters are an advantage. But once you've mastered the leg snap and follow-through required by a kick start, you'll think nothing of it.

All right. The engine's purring; shift is neutral; you're in the saddle, and the jiffy stand is clear. This first exercise, under power, is a very simple one. I'll stand thirty feet in front of you. You are to ride toward me, straight and sedately, and come to a halt right at my feet—please, without knocking me down.

For this operation, think of three controls *only*. They are: (1) clutch; (2) throttle; and (3) brakes.

Squeeze the left hand-lever flush to the handlebar and you have let "out" the clutch: You've disengaged it from the engine. When you release the lever to its usual position, you have let "in" the clutch: It will engage the engine. The engagement is completed only when the gear has been shifted to a running position such as first, second, and so forth.

You speed the engine by twisting the right-hand grip toward you, counterclockwise. To slow the motor, twist in the opposite direction. However, most throttles have a so-called "dead man's" return spring, automatically idling the engine when the rider's hand is removed.

Ready now. Depress the clutch lever and hold it down as you shift to first. Very delicately, let in the clutch at the same time as you add "revs" to the engine via the throttle. Feel your way by fractions of an inch. Do nothing abruptly. "Feathering" your clutch in this fashion, you can, in fact, move the bike just a foot or so at intervals. Soon you'll catch onto the all-important exact coordination between clutch and throttle.

Good. I'll trust you to perform the exercise. No screeching blast-offs, please. Just come across the thirty feet of ground toward me, in first only, both feet up, on pegs, smoothly under control, and brake smoothly to the mark, with the clutch "out" once again. We'll work on this technique until it's second nature to you, adding left- and right-hand turns, circles and figure 8s, to relieve the monotony.

When you can do it all confidently without boo-boos, you've finished the giant step. Learning to upshift into second—to third—and on up to whatever your top gear position is, should come easily. For example, as you approach the top-out speed for first gear, let out the clutch by depressing the lever, make your shift, then let in the clutch again smoothly. Repeat the procedure, similarly, all the way up to your cruising gear level.

There is a matching engine speed for each gear setting. Feel for it with your throttle. Make a mental note of it and put it into your routine operation.

Downshifting (dropping from fourth to third to second, etc.) requires the same coordination. Slack off the throttle. Clutch out. Shift down a notch. Clutch in. And so on down to first. Always set the throttle for the proper, matching engine speed. You will feel or hear indications if things aren't right, with a little experience.

For instance, make suitable adjustments when gears clash or grind. Downshift when you note the motor laboring or lugging under an overload going slowly at too high a gear position. Shift up when you hear your "mill" whining at a road speed too high for a low gear. Be sensitive to these things and your bike will give you longer, trouble-free performance.

Before riding out of the training area on your own, you ought to practice other "real life" situations. Signal your turns and stops by hand, or with blinkers if you're thus equipped.

Try riding on tricky surfaces, such as sand, gravel, or mud. Ease yourself and your bike through some tight "squeaks," like a narrow path between trees or similar obstructions. On a sloped area, make a complete stop, then start rolling again. Do it both uphill and downhill. This is a good way to discover your "resting leg," that is, the foot to put on the ground for a temporary stop. Usually it's the foot you use to shift gears. Use the same foot every time.

Drill in parking, shutting off, and securing your bike may sound silly. It will until the day your mount falls over, gets mangled, or is stolen. Get into the happy habit of shutting off everything, including gas. Find a solid spot where the stand won't sink in and dump the machine. By all means, cable or chain your charger to a post or what-have-you if you can't keep an eye on it. The bike rustlers are very busy these days.

Finally, as you prepare to ride off for some actual experience on the highway, paste a few life-saving tips in your helmet:

1. In traffic, "advertise" you're there, with bright clothing, reflectors, and a prominent position that makes you easy to see for other motorists. Don't be bashful about riding with your headlights turned on in the daytime—especially in heavy traffic.

2. Don't snuggle up to other vehicles or the road shoulder. Ride for wide clearance, fore, aft, and sideways. Keep a safety "island" all around you.

3. Watch the pavement and act accordingly for potholes, loose stuff, ice, and wet, slick spots. Slow down: Lower gears generally offer better control. Be especially wary of gratings used on some bridges, really bad news for two-wheelers.

4. Think ahead constantly. What's the other guy going to do? What's hiding behind that big truck? What booby trap may be waiting around this next curve? What's my next move?

5. Think happy. Keep your cool, even if other drivers are "clowns" or thoughtless. Use only your rightful share of the road. Surprise everyone with your courteous, heads-up riding.

All the rules add up to one main idea, illustrated by a saying that goes like this: "There are old riders, and there are bold riders. But there are no old, bold riders." In other words, the hot rocks and show-offs just don't last.

But hang in there. We can escape from the bumper-to-bumper brigade. There are places and occasions waiting for you to do all the hard, fast, hairy biking you can take.

FOOTPEG POINTERS

Safety officials prescribe pegs for both the operator and passenger. The gadgets do much more than rest the feet and keep them from tangling in wheel spokes. They play a vital role in several functions of bike control. As a "floor" for the rider's feet, they enable him to shift his weight delicately and thus make precise changes in direction. Pegs also serve as guides and leverage points for pressing either one of the controls operated by the feet.

An excellent technique in off-road riding is to stand upright on the pegs when crossing a stretch of loose, "skittery" material. By dropping his body weight to the pegs, the rider thus lowers the center of gravity. The bike is less likely to topple or break away from traction.

Special pegs having nonskid surfaces are often installed for long

Standing on the pegs automatically lowers the center of gravity and allows better control for the off-road "flier." *Hodaka Photo.*

periods of stand-up riding such as enduros and motocross events. Pegs that fold when struck and that snap back into position by means of return springs are common on many dirt bikes. Riders who object to this method sometimes install pegs of metal that bend on encountering a rock, tree, etc. This gives more protection, they feel, and less likelihood of battered toes.

Finally, pegs are the solid bases from which to clamp the knees firmly against the tank, in order to take command of your charger at full gallop.

FINGER CONTROL

A motorcyclist in action has very busy hands. From a distance, it may appear that both hands are simply gripping and working the handlebar. A close-up look will show that, at times, hands and all fingers and both thumbs are doing many things at once.

For instance, the left thumb and palm may be anchored to the grip, while four fingers are extended and pumping the clutch lever. Or fingers may simply be resting on the lever, alert to a sudden need to disengage gears.

Getting over a small obstacle such as a log is a technique that should be well practiced before heading for back country. *Bernhard A. Roth Photo.*

While this is going on, the right hand may be performing several functions in unison with the left hand. All in the same operation, the right hand can be steadying the handlebar; twisting the throttle grip closed or open; working the front brake-lever—or simply riding the lever in case it's needed quickly. This means dividing the work. Normally, the right thumb and index finger combine to do the throttling and steadying; remaining fingers clench and release the front brake-lever.

Although this rundown sounds like a lesson in playing the piano, it really isn't that complex. Most learners work out their own hands-and-fingers techniques instinctively and rarely have to think about it thereafter.

Worth thinking about, though, is the fact that the design and location of handlebars, grips, and levers must suit the physical convenience of the individual. At all times, he'll definitely want his "hands full" of *100 percent* motorcycle control.

Helmet Hints

The most common article of "uniform" worn by cyclists and other motor sportsmen is the safety helmet. In case you're in an accident, this item has three main jobs to do for you. It lessens the possibility that you may (1) damage your brain; (2) fracture your skull; and/or (3) break your neck.

Many helmet-makers submit to tests guaranteeing that their headpieces truly give riders the required protection. Tests are supervised by several organizations. They see to it that methods are fair and results are accurate.

For example, there is the Safety Helmet Council of America (SHCA), headquartered at Beverly Hills, California. Anyone seeking SHCA certification must furnish four sample helmets of any given model.

Then an independent laboratory takes three of the helmets, and puts one in a freezer; another in a hot oven; and the third completely in water. The fourth is left as is. Each of the four helmets is "punished" in the lab by mechanical weights, hammers, and punches. Effects are recorded. The aim is to find out if the headpieces measure up to standards set for (1) reducing shock to the brain; (2) withstanding penetration by sharp objects; and (3)

Helmet and face shield, recommended headgear for the two-wheel rider who prefers this device over a standard shield. *Bell Photo.*

strength of fasteners meant to keep the helmet on the head during an accident.

No helmet may have an outside projection, such as a snap or strapkeeper, greater than three-sixteenths inch. The idea is to prevent the helmet's snagging on anything, if you were to be thrown from your machine to slide on a roadway, embankment, etc. (The

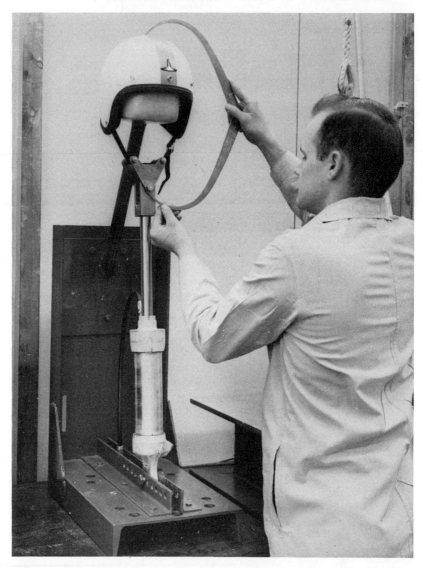

Helmet manufacturers use exacting tests to make sure that the headgear is thoroughly safe under a variety of conditions. *Dayton Brown Company Photo.*

slide might injure you; but the violent snagging of your head could be fatal.)

Manufacturers of helmets that survive the lab examination are permitted to use the yellow-and-black SHCA certification mark—

on tested models only. To make sure the quality is upheld, SHCA may, at any time and anywhere, buy helmets off the shelf without warning. If these fail the lab tests, the manufacturer loses his certification privileges.

The general purpose of SHCA and similar groups is to help the riders, racing officials, and motor vehicle agencies to identify and select helmets that afford known degrees of protection.

IN DEFENSE OF THE HEAD

A continuing argument as to whether so-called "helmet laws" are fair to cyclists may rage on forever. Some feel that they are being "picked on" for regulations not applied to other kinds of motorists. Meanwhile, accident figures indicate that most motorcycling deaths do result from head injuries. For that reason, nearly all experienced riders agree that putting on the "dome defender" is smart—law or no law.

In support of this outlook, SHCA says that although the "Z90 Standard" ("Z90" is motorcyclist jargon referring to a particular research project done for the safety helmet industry. Resulting recommendations were catalogued as "Z90.1—1966," *Specifications for Protective Headgear for Vehicular Users,* published by United States of America Standards Institute, New York) is the highest in the world, it is still a *minimum.* "The shock absorption test is related to an impact at 13 *miles per hour.* This means that any rider whose head strikes an object at a greater speed may not live to tell the story, even if his helmet has passed the test."

Summing it up, SHCA says: "Considering these facts, should anyone who is planning a safety helmet for use during any type of motorsport activity choose a helmet which does NOT *exceed* requirements of the Standard? There can be only one answer and that is *NO!*"

With that concept in mind, there seems little room to debate if a head is worth *at least* twenty to twenty-five dollars to its owner.

"USED" HELMETS NO BARGAIN

"The Society of Used Helmets" could be the name of a non-existent organization no one wants to join. It's composed of riders

A tinted face shield that snaps onto the helmet is a great aid in reducing glare. Avoid dense colors that obscure traffic light signals or make night riding dangerous. *Ed. De Rienze Photo.*

whose helmets saved them from bodily harm or worse. Members of the group aren't exactly proud of their scarred headpieces—just grateful.

We've been shown such souvenirs and marveled at the life-saving jobs they obviously performed. One that revealed massive gouging on the outer shell is owned by a fellow who barreled into a deer

at about 50 mph—after dark. The deer was transformed into veni-
son steaks. The rider absorbed bruises, scrapes, and some cracked
ribs.

Another helmet we recall had its outer layer cracked from crown
to brim. It cushioned its owner's fall after a flight through the air.
The flight followed a broadside collision with an auto that shot
out of a side road. Again, the rider escaped serious injury.

Both headpieces were immediately retired from active duty and
new toppers purchased. This matches advice offered by helmet
safety organizations. Any helmet known to have suffered rough
treatment is a poor risk. Even if it appears okay to the eye, it
should be rigorously tested before being worn again.

ANCIENTS ENCASED THEIR NOGGINS

Modern cycle safety helmets trace back at least twenty-five
hundred years. Long ago Persians and Assyrians wore headgear of
leather and iron in the Battle of Marathon in Greece in 490 B.C.
The Safety Helmet Council of America says that ancient Greeks
and Romans bedecked their helmets with baubles, bangles, and
plumes. Through the Middle Ages, war helms began to assume
the contours of the human head. This shows in streamlined designs now used by military and police units.

Europeans led the way to head-savers for motor sportsmen. The
famous automobile speedster of England, Sir Malcolm Campbell,
presented an early-model helmet to the ace American driver, Wil-
bur Shaw, in 1932. Almost immediately, it was credited with saving Shaw's life. Soon thereafter, helmets for American race drivers
became mandatory.

In 1955, the Los Angeles Police Department became the first
user of safety helmets for motorcycle-mounted officers. Since 1966,
vehicle-headgear makers have largely heeded advice issued by the
United States of America Standards Institute. Protection beyond
the minimum is built into many "approved" motorcycling helmets
today.

The Two-Wheeled World Around You

Congratulations. You passed your operator's test. At last you're free to ride the highways and byways on your own. You can gun your colorful machine in any direction you choose—discover for yourself all the pleasures and excitement open to you and millions of fellow cyclists.

Maybe you aren't exactly prepared for this sudden freedom. What does a motorcyclist do? Sure, he or she *rides*—you can bet your motocross boots on that. But where? When? And what's at the end of the ride?

PLEASURE RUN

Every new rider does his share of hitting the "glory trail" around town or the neighborhood. It's only natural to show the crowd your rolling bronc and hard-won skill. And it often jogs friends into joining you in two-wheel sport. Soon, though, you'll tire of droning past the library for the umpteenth time. The open road—away from traffic—will tug at your handlebars.

So select a point of interest, and scheme the best, most pleasant route to take you there and back. Zero in on some place worthwhile: the home of a friend or relative to whom you owe a visit; a mountain lake or stream; a game refuge; a hill with a scenic view;

an outdoor recreation area; a farm or ranch community; a fishing village; and so on and on. Part of the fun is planning the run carefully with a target in mind. You won't be wobbling around, undecided, at intersections. Beforehand, you'll know which roads will take you out of the bumper-to-bumper-to-bumper drag and confusion.

Two to three hours on the road make a nice round-trip run. Or settle for an hour, if that's all you've got. When you reach your outbound destination, dismount and do something. Deliver an item; take a picture; make a note in your diary; say hello; pick up a souvenir; have a Coke; watch a cycle sport event.

The main idea is that you get in the habit of piloting your bike, rather than simply having it haul you around. There's a difference —and you'll enjoy it. And "leg-stretching" runs are good for the machine. Your friendly cycle mechanic will advise you that bikes thrive on healthy exercise.

A bike's ability to go practically anywhere was demonstrated by Englishman Paul Pratt with a Triumph 650cc shown at San Blas in a Panamanian jungle during a forty-thousand-mile tour of Central America. *Triumph Photo.*

TOURING

Nothing beats the thrill of swinging out of the driveway toting luggage to keep you wheeling for several days or longer. You'll want a machine that will carry the load in comfort, and safely, at today's highway speeds. Planning of the route, overnight stops, equipment needed, and the trip budget are important. In case of emergency, it's a good idea to give the folks at home your itinerary and keep in touch as you proceed.

With a few common-sense limitations, it's possible to cycle overland to almost any spot on earth. The jungle, desert, plains, subarctic, and many of the world's highest mountains have all been conquered by motorcyclists. From such experiences, manufacturers have learned much that helps them make the vehicles ever more rugged and dependable.

A long weekend or perhaps a week's vacation is plenty adventurous for many touring riders. Medium-to-heavyweight bikes are usually the choice for transporting the tourist and all necessary travel and recreation gear.

There's a good rule of thumb: A bike will handle almost anything that you can attach to it *securely*, and that doesn't get in the way of *safe operation*. Remember that ample *power* is part of safety. Test to be sure you have enough for the load. Thus the tourist can shove off well set up for tenting, hunting, and fishing, with a range of clothing to match rain, sun, or frost. For example, the author, at times, totes a twelve-foot canoe. Of course it's inflatable, and it deflates and packs to about the size of a bedroll.

Don't overlook your bike's ability to propel you way out yonder, for fascinating days on end, and at moderate costs that won't flatten your wallet. Your dollar will take you two to three times farther than the ordinary motorist can stretch his buck.

GROUP RIDING

Membership in a well-organized motorcycle club is an excellent means of answering where-to-go and what-to-do hangups. Regular weekly rides are usually scheduled well ahead, over routes tested

A secluded fishing spot a few hours' ride from home is one way to make the outdoor scene. This is in Spain. *Bultaco Photo.*

and proven to be interesting and safe. There is a special thrill and satisfaction in riding as a group. Special rules and signals are needed to protect individuals riding in the formation and to guard the safety of other motorists sharing the road.

Favorite objectives for many club rides are the hundreds of cycle-sport events held throughout the United States on any given Sunday afternoon. These are uniformly regulated to provide fair, clean, wholesome competition. Common events are scrambles, hill climbs, flat tracks, enduros, road races, motocross, trials, drags, and others described elsewhere in this book.

Those who enter must submit their machines to rigid inspection for safety. However, there's a lot of fun and education to be gained by just witnessing rider skill and bike performance at their finest.

Other high spots on club riding calendars are games that can be played in areas as small as an ordinary parking lot. An entire day of contests, with prizes and a wiener roast thrown in, may be devoted to good-humored rider-testing such as "slow time" races,

Whether for hunting, shooting, or fishing, the sports-minded cyclist can use his machine in all types of terrain and even through water. *BSA Company Photo.*

hanging-out-the-washing, teeterboard, limbo ride, figure-8 slalom, and so on.

Join the group—for that extra flavor awheel.

SHOPPING AROUND

Still another activity that involves riding with a mission in mind might be called "cycle shop snooping." The object is to get acquainted with a goodly number of the reputable dealers and suppliers in your general area. Track them down through the Yellow Pages, newspaper and magazine ads, and by asking fellow riders.

Personal visits are the best means of discovering where the various makes, parts, accessories, and services are located. You may need the information some day when you're in a hurry to solve a special problem. The average cycle shop is not a big operation and seldom has all the gadgets and all the know-how. Be prepared to put the finger quickly on who can do what for you.

Shop snooping is an ideal way to widen your circle of friendships among motorcycle businessmen of the community. Also, you're sure to meet other riding enthusiasts—fellows and girls who'll be shopping around for the same reasons you have.

ROUND THE CLOCK

Even when you're not actually in the saddle, there are plenty of nonriding activities that could fill every hour in your day—certainly more time than you can spare from school, work, and other vital things. The possibilities suit nearly any taste.

Some fans try to see every cycle-related movie that comes to town or that appears on local television. The quality of the productions varies from good to indifferent, and some are real clunkers. But they improve as producers learn more about the machines and riders. There is a certain amount of interest in seeing the kinds of bikes filmed, and how producers dramatize the sport.

Collecting personal libraries of photos, artwork, catalogs, magazines, and books is another avenue to interesting hobbies in the cycle field. Reading about the wide world of bikedom is a rewarding hobby in itself. Literature about the sport constantly grows in coverage and color, around the world.

Possibly no pastime is more popular among riders than plain, ordinary "cycle watching." All you need is a sharp eye and your natural curiosity about anything motorized on two wheels. Simply observe the kinds of bikes used by mounted police, messenger servicemen, warehouse yard workers, and any wayfaring stranger who wheels into view. Collar the rider on an unfamiliar model and get him to identify his machine and tell you all about it. The chances are the rider will be more than delighted to oblige. Most cyclists are cycle watchers, too.

Ride Friendly

Light rain began to hit me as I rode into a small town in southern New Jersey just at dusk. I rented a room in the town's one hotel, but was disappointed to learn it had no garage or parking space for the bike. "You can park it in that municipal lot down the street," said the clerk.

Like most riders, I'm not happy to leave a bike alone in a strange place. But there was no choice. Rain was falling harder as I backtrailed down the street. I snapped on my headlights as I crossed the oncoming traffic lane into the lot. Killing my engine and lights and cutting the gas, I spotted a big roadbike hulking under tarpaulin in a nearby slot. At that moment, a door slammed at the rear of a supermarket alongside of the lot and a helmeted figure came bounding toward me.

"Here, use my tarp if you're going to stay overnight," called the helmet wearer. I had barely opened my mouth to say thanks when he hauled the canvas off of his machine and threw it over mine. Jumping into the saddle, he kicked his starter, caught the ignition on the first throw, and yelled at me over the rumble of his engine. "No sense of us both getting wet. Gotta get home. Put the tarp in that shed back of the store if you leave real early. If you don't, I'll see you here at eight-thirty in the morning. I have to be back of the meat counter again at nine!" He geared away into the wet darkness with a parting wave of his hand.

I met the local rider bright and early the next day. Together, we throttled through the narrow, twisting streets. Then he led me over a quick shortcut to the highway that would take me home. At the access ramp, my guide swung around and grinned over his idling motor. "We cyclists have got to stick together, right?" "Right!" I yelled. And we parted.

Friendliness is a natural thing among motorcyclists. You will find this generally true of riders the world over. My own interest in cycling has put me on instant good terms with fellow enthusiasts in many places, in the jungles of Pacific islands, across the United States, in rural Ireland, and in the industrial cities of West Germany.

FRIEND MAKER

Arriving on any scene aboard a motorcycle seems to be a sure way to start friendly conversations with people who mightn't otherwise say hello.

Wheel into just about any diner, filling station, or crossroads store, and almost always, someone will strike up a chat with you. Perhaps it's because the bike is still a long shot from being a "common-ordinary" vehicle. The machine and its rider arouse curiosity in many areas at home and abroad.

Strangers seem prone to think a cyclist must have some interesting experiences to relate. They'll ask you how far and how fast you've come—the miles per gallon you get—and if a bike is dangerous.

On rainy days you'll be asked how you keep dry. In wintry weather you'll surely hear somebody say: Doesn't it get a little snappy on that thing? Whatever the opening sally, it's a good excuse for the cyclist to take his own turn sounding out the local news, best roads to take, and other helpful information.

Among riders themselves, there's a comradeship that's rare with other operators awheel. Its common expression is a quick wave of the left hand whenever riders pass on the open road. In a split

Take to the woods on a motorcycle. Effective mufflers and spark arresters are a must. *Yamaha Photo.*

second it says a lot, including, "Hi, buddy—glad you like bikes—happy riding to you!"

There are individuals who spoil the average cyclist's reputation as a good sportsman. They are rightly called "outlaws" because of their trouble-making behavior. Unfortunately, some movies, magazines, and newspapers play up these characters for headline values. But, fortunately, the "saddle bums" are actually few in number. They are not genuine cyclists and seldom own a machine more than a short while before they tire of it. Then they switch to spoiling fun in another activity.

Young folks who enjoy cycling purely as a fun way to travel can help correct the impression created by outlaws. The best method is to ride strictly according to traffic rules; keep cycles and riding clothes neat and sharp; and miss no opportunity to show friendliness to one and all.

Membership in one of the thousands of community motorcycle clubs in the United States is often a means of helping the sport.

Organized riders frequently put on shows to demonstrate their interest in road safety, charity campaigns, and community activities such as rescue squads, blood banks, and volunteer fire departments. The motorcycle is an attractive vehicle; and the public does turn out to see the skills of riding in formation, doing figure 8s, playing cycle polo, and so on.

Many clubs encourage members to go to the aid of other motorists in distress, including four-wheeled travelers. A friend of mine endorses this idea from personal experience.

Halfway around a sharp, blind curve on a back-country road, he was suddenly confronted with the rear end of a stalled car. Panic-braking, he was able to lay his machine over without damage, on the grassy shoulder. In the car he found a flustered woman with her two impatient children.

"The car just stopped dead," said the woman. "I don't know what to do." My friend checked the gas gauge and then—just to be sure—the float bowl of the carburetor. His suspicions confirmed, he wheeled back to the nearest service station and arranged to have a can of fuel delivered. He lingered to be certain the woman and youngsters got rolling again.

A few days later, my friend was pleasantly startled when the hometown newspaper carried a letter to the editor reading: "I'd like to publicly thank the friendly motorcyclist who helped me get my car started on Reservoir Road last Wednesday morning. He was a real gentleman and I'm sorry I was so excited I forgot to get his name. I know cyclists get blamed for a lot of things. I want to say I met a 'good guy' and I suspect there must be others." Signed by the grateful mother.

Although motorcycling is having its biggest boom in American history, two-wheelers are far outnumbered by the millions of cars and trucks on the highway. This means that millions of motorists don't understand cycles. And they have mixed-up impressions of the kind of people who ride them.

Every rider can share the big job of educating the public, to close the gap in understanding. One way to do it is to heed an old saying among veterans of the saddle: "Put your friendliest wheel forward."

Minis Are Many

Things are humming in the mini field. Over six hundred thousand mini machines were sold in a recent year, according to the Recreation Off-Road Vehicles of America Corporation. At least two million of them are stowed in backyards, campers, or car trunks right now—or buzzing around a parking lot, sand pit, or woodland trail.

Less than 10 percent are ever registered for use on public roads. So it's difficult to keep track of where the minis are, who owns them, and what they do with them. Piecemeal information from police, safety officials, the minibike industry, and the press adds up to a cloudy picture. The little vehicle's proper place in the scene hasn't yet been figured out.

There's some good news. If you're in the nine-to-fifteen-year age bracket, here's a great chance to get years of riding experience before you're old enough to go "street legal." On the problem side, youngsters are getting killed riding illegally in high-speed public road traffic. There's a pressing demand for safe, off-road miniriding areas for public use.

And pint-sized beginners need veteran leaders to show them that biking can be danger-free, and fun, too. Plenty of adult novices, too, are among the mini fans.

Los Angeles Northeast YMCA Y-riders get a briefing on maneuvers to be followed around pylons from fellow members as part of the youth assistance project sponsored in cooperation with the American Honda Motor Company. *NYPUM Photo.*

WHAT'S A MINI?

Two breeds of mini are generally recognized by the industry. One is the *minibike*. The other is the *minicycle*. Common features occur in both. Therefore, don't expect a perfect definition. Differences between the two are very general, as follows:

Mini*bikes* average smaller in most dimensions; have fewer refinements in drive systems and suspension; and rarely have front brakes, lights, etc., that can pass state inspection. Typically, they're powered by small industrial engines, originally designed for mowers, electric generators, and so on.

Easy to carry, simple to operate, and inexpensive to buy, the basic no-extras minibike sells in greatest numbers. It's the camper's favorite, and most often the fledgling rider's pride and joy.

Mini*cycles*, on the other hand, usually feature the dash, styling,

Minicycles are just the right size for the young rider, giving him years of experience before going "street legal." *Montesa Photo.*

and advanced components of full-size bikes. They *look* like motor-cycles, although somewhat shrunken. They handle much like adult models, with elaborate suspension, "grown-up" drive systems, competition features, and brake/light/horn, etc., fittings that can be licensed for public road use.

In contrast to the minibike, most minicycles are powered by scaled-down but true motorcycle engines, rather than adapted industrial units. Some mills are actually full-scale. They are by no means "mini" in performance. Watch a Junior Class race in scrambles or motocross. It's the *real thing*.

More manufacturers are going into the minicycle type of production. The design has instant appeal for families who do their riding together. When Brother and Sis whisk alongside on flashy replicas of trail cycles ridden by Mom and Dad, togetherness goes into high gear.

Some of the new minitrail and minienduro entries can in fact serve adults fairly well. Their performance dampens when the rider's weight goes much beyond 125 pounds; but they'll "get there and back," as the saying goes.

Generally, all minis tend to bog down under riders of big adult weight: 150 pounds and more. Riding them "double up" under any circumstances is a sure recipe for breakdowns or accidents.

We know an entire dealer staff of eight people—all experienced motorcycle riders—each of whom was "bitten" by minibikes. They have scars to prove it. In most of their accidents, the tiny buzz-bombs simply "squirted" out from under their adult-size bulk and beef.

STYLISH HARDWARE

Mini activities extend well beyond the around-the-camp and around-the-yard orbit. Schoolboy and -girl riders now take their place in special "vest pocket" events. They, too, have their own cheering sections every Sunday throughout the competition circuit.

Already, four national short track championships combining minibikes and minicycles have been held. Entrants have numbered as many as two hundred annually, featuring riders six years old on

Ready for a training ride. The small size of the mini is ideal for young group riders. The bikes are Honda Mini-Trails donated to the National Youth Project. *NYPUM Photo.*

up to adults. An increasing number of girls ride the always popular "powder puff" events. Just as in the big-time race meetings, there's a lovely young trophy queen to award prizes and give the boys a smack. Winning machines bear some of the proudest names in the senior cycle industry, along with dozens of firm names allied only to minispecialty production.

The will-to-win among the midgets has opened the door to mechanical refinements paralleling those in big bikes. For instance, in minispeed equipment alone, you'll find a practically endless array of "goodies," including fuel injection; unbreakable connecting rods; racing style camshafts; extra-capacity carburetors; high-compression engine heads; and high-tension valve springs, among others.

Special tires and wheels; front and rear suspensions to suit all rider specialties—these too can be found on regular stock machines, or available for custom fitting.

As to drive systems, minis have the "works": three basic devices, plus varieties of each. The three are: centrifugal clutch—controlled by the throttle; clutch and gearbox—the hand-and-foot-operated arrangement used on most motorcycles; and the torque converter—an automatic transmission that compares with automobile designs.

Torque converters have mechanisms that constantly select the correct gear ratio. One type senses the "right" gear by the speed of the engine. Another type reacts to the load being put upon the drive system—that is, the energy demanded for the particular hill, sandwash, or what have you.

A converter relieves the rider of constantly shifting up and down, which is quite a chore in a hectic race. The advantages of applying this same idea to the larger cycles are being checked by designers. There are technical problems, but the minis may yet be credited with showing the way. Meanwhile, the newer midget models are being equipped with improved silencers, emission controls, and spark arresters, to make them more acceptable in the wildwoods and suburban neighborhoods.

LITTLE BIKES HELP YOUTH

Minibike riding as a method of helping young folks in trouble is being promoted by the Motorcycle Industry Council. An example is the National Youth Project Using Mini-Bikes (NYPUM) initiated by the American Honda Motor Company. Honda offered to donate ten thousand of its Mini-Trail models. Members of the Safety Helmet Council of America agreed to supply as many helmets at cost. Then federal justice agencies assigned funds to help employ local leaders.

The national organization of YMCAs accepted the challenge to get activities going in live-wire communities. Beginning with a trial project at the Northeast YMCA in Los Angeles, NYPUM's units spread like wildfire. At more than a hundred locations around the country, kids eleven to fifteen years old get together and learn rider skills, safety, and bike mechanics. With older fellows guiding them, they pretty much run their own programs. Several hours a week, they practice maneuvers on parking lots and playgrounds, or discuss cycling know-how indoors. Often they're transported to the hinterlands for dirt-rider training. Trips are aided by police, civic officials, and service clubs in communitywide efforts.

Many of the youngsters have had previous troubles with the law, school authorities, and parents. There's evidence that minibikes are helping them discover a worthwhile outlet for their energies. There are very few dropouts.

Fred Hoshiyama, who directs NYPUM from the Los Angeles headquarters, said, "We have new local projects starting each week, so that it's hard to give an accurate count. Many have been approved and are ready to go, awaiting a shipment of bikes, which takes two to three weeks from the time of ordering."

With two million dollars' worth of Mini-Trails on tap, the project can eventually introduce as many as twenty thousand youngsters to the saddle each year. One youthful "Y" rider gave his personal thoughts: "Riding a minibike is a great thing because it's exciting fun, and most of all, it gives you a sense of being free. . . . You can just hop on and take off going nowhere and everywhere, just following a trail wherever it leads."

GROWTH UNLIMITED

Minis are beginning to play an important role in public education for motorcycling. A good example was the Mini-Bike Rodeo held at a Lancaster, Pennsylvania, junior high, by the Student Organization for Safety.

Twenty-five boys competed in events that included a custom show; serpentine run; racing around pylons and cloverleafs; a plank-balancing marathon; and drag eliminations. Seventh-, eighth-, and ninth-graders from the Wheatland School showed spectators they could "get it all together" in minibike skills, thrills, and safety. Their program won the endorsement of the Lancaster City School District. Educators agreed that with good planning and plenty of common sense, miniriding's future has real promise.

Officials of the National Safety Council added their comment: "Minibikes need not be as dangerous as they have proved to be when misused. In fact, they can help young people develop manual dexterity, coordination, judgment, and a feeling for a driving situ-

ation that may aid them when they begin to operate street vehicles.

"A safety program that combines responsible riding with fun
can eliminate many fatalities that occur when minibikes are misused by untrained, unsupervised children."

The Scooter Story

Scooters have helped set the stage for two-wheeled motoring in America. Many a GI in the Occupation forces after World War II caught the scootering "bug" and brought it home from Europe. Europeans developed the vehicle from a rather primitive toy into a reliable means of transportation. Many war-torn countries badly needed it. Italy, with its excellent, stylish Vespa and Lambretta models, found eager buyers at home and all over the world, including Asia. Manufacturers in France, England, Austria, Germany, and Czechoslovakia quickly followed suit.

In the 1950s, at least fifty different scooter models were flitting around the American scene. Besides the ex-GIs, college students, businessmen, housewives, and outdoor enthusiasts delighted in this cheap, fun way of getting about.

Sleek automotive styling, colorful trim, and impressive performance helped the scooter win a considerable following. Models having improved engines, modern gear-systems, big wheels, and elaborate suspension approached the speeds and reliability of motorcycles. One such was made by Heinkel, the German aircraft company. Other scooter makes that have been sold on the American market in fair numbers are: NSU; Cushman; Allstate; Maicoletta; Zundapp; BSA; Progress; Cosmo; TWN; Parilla; Peugeot;

The motor scooter's adaptability to carrying peak loads of equipment is apparent as two riders prepare for a lightweight camping trip. These are Vespa 150cc's. *G. Smith Photo.*

and Harley-Davidson. Many older machines are still running well, although no longer marketed.

Some appear, from time to time, in the used bike ads. Unless you are a two-wheel antique collector or an advanced mechanic, take care. Getting parts and service may be a real ordeal.

Since the early 1960s, the scooter's future in the United States has been uncertain. One of its original sales points, that of a "second car in the family," has dimmed. Americans actually tend to buy the second car and often the third car, instead. For two-wheeling as a sport activity, preference has swung toward conventional motorcycles plus "vest pocket" bikes or cycles in the numerous minisizes.

Yet, the motor scooter, in its own way, is a remarkable performer. The vehicle continues to give vital service to millions on the Continent and in the Far East. As you begin cycling, you may find a scooter worth considering for your special needs.

The scooter's floor board and protective cowling are unique features among two-wheelers. This vehicle's popularity continues high among Europeans and among less-developed nations around the world. This is a Lambretta 150cc motor scooter. *G. Smith Photo.*

Motor scooters can be compared to motorcycles and other two-wheelers in certain respects. But a number of scooter features are truly unique. Convenience is, so to speak, this vehicle's name.

The scooter engine is generally placed beneath and somewhat

behind the rider. The operator steps aboard with ease, places his feet on the floorboard, and takes a seat as in a chair.

A cowling usually encloses all working parts. This includes a wide metal shield over the front fork. The result is a sort of cockpit, offering protection and comfort. Splashing mud and water rarely affect the rider. With a windshield added, the machine gives cozy shelter, like a cab.

These automotive-style benefits are often fully utilized abroad. An entire family—mother, father, and several children—may be seen traveling on board a single scooter. This is not an unusual sight in such countries as Italy, Greece, Indonesia, and the Malay states. The bodywork affords generous storage and carrying of luggage and tools. In this capacity, the scooter surpasses other two-wheelers.

Since most scooters have been designed for family "knock-about" usage, foolproof reliability and economic operation are apparent. The majority have simple, two-stroke engines in the 50cc to 150cc sizes. Coupled with relatively lightweight body components, they often deliver excellent utility at quite modest cost.

In sophisticated designs, motor scooters give riders a wide range of attractions, including electric starters, battery-powered lights, full shock-absorbent suspension, spare wheels and spare tires, fuel gauges, gear-phase indicators, passenger seats, spare fuel tanks, multicolor selections in paint trim, and several choices in drive-train mechanisms. For example, there are models driven by chains; by shafts; and by a system of gears working between the engine and the rear drive-wheel. The latter method was devised by Vespa, and accounts for the bulbous shape at the tail section of this well-known runabout.

Criticisms of the motor scooter have some basis in fact, but depend upon which model is being cited. Small wheels and tires with minimum—and insecure—traction on the road have typified some scooter designs. Yet there are also models with big (sixteen-inch) wheels that compare with motorcycles in good traction and safety. A generally higher seating position may account for topheaviness in the machine sometimes mentioned by critics.

A motor scooterist made the distance from Pennsylvania to the Bay of Fundy in Nova Scotia on his Vespa 150cc. *Bernhard A. Roth Photo.*

There have been complaints of inadequate power. Engines tend to be small, but the horsepower-to-weight ratio in scooters is often favorable. It seems likely that scooterists often take on greater loads than their mounts were designed to handle.

In short, the scooter is a specialist. Its best role is probably that of a quick, convenient, round-the-town commuter and shopper— even though adventurers have long since ridden the breed to the far corners of the world. At least once in your two-wheeled life-time, give scootering a whirl. It's "different."

The Rider's a Mechanic

Give your rugged, modern motorcycle half a chance. It will rumble happily over the many thousand miles for which it was designed. There are a number of things you can do, yourself, to keep on rolling. Although today's bike is built to "take it," give it regular care. Day after day of trouble-free riding will be guaranteed.

Most cyclists enjoy the simple upkeep chores, much as a cowboy takes pleasure feeding and watering Old Paint. If you like tinkering with a purpose, you've picked the right sport. Skill by skill, you may work up to becoming an advanced mechanic. Many long-time cyclists are.

Sparkle plenty: The very least you can do for your mount is to free it of mud, dust, grease, and grime once a week. Use water, cleansers, and sponges—the same materials you use on the family car. Spray on "gunk," a special solvent to help get rid of clinging grease. Apply a moist chamois cloth to avoid leaving dry streaks on the paint finish. Clean tail- and headlight lenses with regular window-washing fluid. Plastic (plexiglass) windshields take a special cleanser. All items can be gotten at any auto or cycle supply store.

Why blitz up, except for looks? For one thing, you'll be reducing dirt that works into—and ruins—vital parts and accessories. Also,

The cycle owner's bag of tricks should include knowing how to make road-side repairs and adjustments. *R. Roth Photo.*

a bright, shiny machine is more easily seen by other motorists—all the safer for you by night or day.

Owner's manual: Here's your "bible" of instructions on how to keep your bike in trim. Insist on your copy if the dealer forgets to hand one over with your new machine. Write to the manufacturer

An inexpensive home-built shed provides all-weather shelter for a trail bike. This is a small investment that lengthens the life of any machine. *Bernhard A. Roth Photo.*

if you don't receive one with a used model. Sit beside the two-wheeler while you study the manual. Reach out and touch the various controls, parts, components, and adjusters, as quickly as you can locate them in the diagrams.

Pay strict attention to the proper gasoline, oil, battery, light bulbs, fuses, nuts, bolts, and whatnot. Memorize whatever you can, but always carry the booklet with you on a ride. Some day, crouched by a lonely roadside, you'll be glad you did!

Tools and other fix-it equipment: For first-aid maintenance, you can manage well with a fistful of selected items. A minimum kit might include (1) a screwdriver; (2) pliers, with wire-cutting edges; (3) an assortment of open-end and Allen-type wrenches, to fit ten or a dozen different-size nuts, bolts, etc.; (4) a crescent adjustable wrench or two, in the four-to-seven-inch range; (5) a chain-repair tool, commonly called a chainbreaker; and (6) feeler gauges—usually two or three, having different thicknesses specified in your manual. Carry them in waterproof wrapping or a case, to prevent rust.

*Good tools cost money. Cheap, ill-made ones will butcher your bike and spoil your sense of humor. Buy quality items, in amounts you can afford, rather than a complete set of junk at a "bargain" price. There's a vast array of ultraspecial tools and aids made to speed and ease the work. You'll have a better idea as to which of these you really need when you've mastered the simpler gadgets.

A means of detecting shortages in your tool kit is the "try on" system. With the kit spread out, examine all fastenings on the cycle. Check to insure you're equipped to manipulate them. Make sure each tool *really* fits. For example, a poor-fitting screwdriver will chew away the slot in the head of a bolt or screw. Sloppily fitting wrenches will wear down nuts to the point that even the "right" wrench won't loosen them.

Gasoline and other fuels: Tanking up with the right grade of gas is smart maintenance. Use what the book says—generally, the "high test" for high-compression, four-stroke engines, and "regular" for lower-compression units. For two-stroke motors, you'll add prescribed oil, either in a separate, automatic-feed reservoir or hand-mixed into the main tank.

A little extra care will help prevent fouling of spark plugs in two-stroke motorcycle and mini-engines. Oil (that is mixed with gasoline) tends to collect on spark plug electrodes when the bike is parked for a long period. An effective remedy is to shut off the fuel line and let the engine run until it burns up all the fuel mix present in the cylinder or cylinders. The next start should be an easy one.

Many station attendants will hand you the hose and let you pump your own gas. That way, you can shut off at the level you know is best. Overfilling, for instance, will have fuel seeping down your legs or over your hot engine, which might cause problems. Do keep "topped up," though, to avoid conking out in an unhandy spot. This also prevents moisture from collecting in your tank.

Oil servicing: Nothing will bring your cycling to a screeching halt faster than neglecting oil requirements. We refer particularly to oil for the engine/gearbox/clutch/transmission system. Here are fast-moving parts working against each other at terrific heat ranges. They simply must have oil to prevent their melting and stopping—and also to prevent wearing out rapidly.

The grade and quality of oil called for in your manual has definite meaning. It will not break down—become thin and watery —at operating temperatures. It will reach all vital parts. It will stay effective during the period between oil changes.

Depending on the bike you're riding, there'll be one to several places on it for oil servicing. Get a spout that fits into a quart can and a small funnel. Add oil as the "good book," your manual, says.

Changing oil is a cinch. Stand the bike upright. Place a drain pan under the drain plug. Remove the plug with a wrench and let the dirty oil drain into a waste pan. Usually there's an oil filter screen attached to the plug. Clean the screen with gasoline or gunk. Reattach the screen and plug. Put in the fresh oil. Bring it up to the level marked on the dipstick. Dispose of waste oil in a manner that avoids polluting the environment.

Whether adding or changing oil, the engine should be warm.

Battery care: Once a month is about the right interval to make sure the battery fluid is up to the proper level. If it is not, add distilled water or whatever is specified, to keep the plates covered. Pick up a "squeeze bulb" battery filler to simplify the job.

Trouble getting the engine started, and dimmer-than-normal

headlights, may be a battery fault. Have its condition tested. Any auto service station can do it. Be sure to tell them the voltage (six or twelve) if not clearly marked on the battery. Batteries incline to go bad when not in use. Follow the special instructions for winter storage. It's cheaper than a brand-new battery.

Tire watching: By all means, get your own pocket-size tire pressure gauge, and use it. Don't depend on the gauge in the air pump at the service station: it's almost never accurate. Correct pressures mean more mileage and a comfortable ride. Your front tire should generally carry less air than the rear one. Amazing is the number of "bumps" this will take out of the road.

Motorcycle tires are fantastically tough. In routine riding, they rarely puncture; blowouts are nearly unheard of. When one wears out, or fails to pass state inspection, your dealer will replace it for the price of the new rubber.

Should you prefer—or be forced—to change a tire, you'll need a set of tire irons. You raise the bike and remove the wheel as indicated in your manual. Remove the nut that secures the valve stem. On some machines, there may also be a "tire security" bolt

Rib or front runner tread for pavement. *Bernhard A. Roth Photo.*

Rib or front runner or speed grip tread for pavement. *Bernhard A. Roth Photo.*

Semiknobby tread for on- and off-road driving. *Bernhard A. Roth Photo.*

Universal tread for on- and off-road driving. *Bernhard A. Roth Photo.*

Full knobby (motocross or trials) treads especially used for off-road driving. *Bernhard A. Roth Photo.*

to be loosened. With the irons, pry tire and tube off, beginning at the side nearest the valve. Inspect the condition of the tube while you have the chance. When remounting tire and tube, start by inserting the area including the valve. Carry a "spare tire in a can." This can of pressurized air will, most often, inflate a soft or flat tire enough to get you to the nearest service station.

\Drive-chain upkeep: Careful lubrication, using a special lube, prevents chain wear and breakage. So does keeping the right amount of "play" in the chain. Check your manual for directions. It will tell you how to slide your rear wheel backward to take up slack; or forward to provide more "play" (looseness). The same directions apply to putting on a new chain.

Repairing a broken chain is messy—but better than walking ten miles or so. A simple break will usually require two master links and a block—plus a so-called chain breaker. When you buy these items, get a friendly mechanic to show you how it's done.

Spark plugs: These are easy to remove and inspect at prescribed times, or whenever you suspect they're causing poor engine performance. Use your spark plug socket wrench. Look for deposits of oil and dirt in the sparking element. Clean by scraping and wiping, or with a sand-blast cleaner found at filling stations. Check for correct gap, using the right size feeler gauge.

Use only the recommended plug for replacement. It will give you the best gas mileage and easiest starting. Put in a new gasket with each new plug. Put plugs back in just firmly—never tighten by brute strength.

Circuit-breaker timing: Part of the ignition system, the circuit-breaker has contact points that control the precise moment that charges of electricity are released to the spark plugs. Plugs "fire off" fuel and air in the engine's combustion chambers. The timing system is set in the factory, and is operated by the engine as it turns over. Engraved markings in the timer case and on the engine's flywheel indicate the right setting.

The procedure for adjustment is spelled out carefully in the owner's manual. It includes setting the correct gap for the breaker points by means of a feeler gauge. Timing is done at long intervals (two thousand miles or so) after a new bike's break-in period.

Spark plug cleaning and gapping is an important owner maintenance chore that should be done when poor ignition is indicated. *R. Roth Photo.*

The technique is not difficult but is "fussy." It may require special equipment.

Lighting system: Burned-out light bulbs and sealed headlight units can be replaced by any rider equipped with a screwdriver. Many imported bikes will accept standard American auto bulbs bought at gas stations. If your bike uses foreign-make items, you had better carry a couple of spares. Be sure to replace six-volt units with six-volt replacements, and twelve-volts units with twelve-volt substitutes. The same is true of electrical fuses; these can be readily snapped in or out of their clips.

Switches that operate your taillight when you apply the brakes occasionally go bad. A suitable wrench will usually loosen the old unit, letting you install the new one.

Major electrical work: Sometime you may have a real puzzler in this department. Nothing you do helps. Avoid costly mistakes. Try no more than the owner's manual indicates. Take the problem to an expert. His know-how and special testing equipment will save you money. This is a better bet than the risk of blowing out your entire expensive electrical system.

Tappet adjustment: This applies to four-stroke engines only. Tappets, in conjunction with the camshaft, make the valves open and close at just the right split-second intervals. Movements must synchronize with the four main positions of the piston in motion: (1) intake of gas and air; (2) compression of gas and air; (3) ignition of the charge; and (4) exhaust of waste gases.

There is a tiny space between the tappet and the valve it operates. This gap must be exact, in thousandths of an inch. The manual tells the gauge size to use, and how to use it.

Generally, the procedure is to remove the spark plug and the "rocker-box cover" that protects the tappets. Rotate the engine to put the piston in the correct position, usually top dead center with valves closed. Loosen tappets (one at a time). Use the gauge to get the right gap, then tighten. Repeat as needed. Replace plug and cover.

Tappet adjustments, except for old or hard-run engines, are seldom needed oftener than two-thousand-mile intervals. Owners of light- and medium-weight motorcycles find the task fairly easy.

Wheels and brakes: A monthly check of your wheels is worth the small effort required. Raise the bike, spin the wheel, and see if it's running true. If it isn't, loosen and jockey the wheel as indicated in the manual until the wheel runs straight, then retighten.

This is a good time to check your brake controls—front and rear—since you'll be working in the same area. Tighten or loosen the brake adjusters. The manual will tell you just how far your hand levers and foot levers should travel for safe braking action. One more check: Are your brake light switches working?

Lubrication: About every thousand miles, your machine should have a complete "lube job" (as well as a change of engine oil). Locate the vital spots in the manual chart. Some of the fittings need grease under pressure. For that, you'll find that a grease gun is a wise buy and is not expensive.

In the same operation, give every exposed nut and bolt a dab of machine oil. There's a reason: Discovering that a fastener is rusted solid is annoying—especially when you're in a hurry. Keep it from happening.

A new machine needs special care at the beginning. Be sure to follow the maker's recommendations. *Ed. De Rienze Photo.*

Preflight habit: Have you noticed that a pilot walks around his airplane, looking at every square inch of it, before getting in? Then he sits in the cockpit and fiddles with all the switches, controls, and instruments for several minutes until he fires up the engine. This "preflight" routine is mighty good practice for motorcyclists.

Running on two wheels only, a bike is actually "flying" to some extent. So always examine your mount before departure. Use the very best tools you will ever have: *your own two bright little eyes!* Look to see if

- chain is oiled and adjusted
- gas and oil are okay
- no nuts and bolts are loose
- your lights work, including brake lights
- your brakes will hold
- tires are inflated correctly
- luggage or bundles are secure
- your clothing, helmet, goggles, or shoes aren't about to come loose

All right, fire up, knock away the stand, *take off, and enjoy!*

Careers for Cyclists

Would you like a job in the motorcycling field? Prospects are good for *specialists* trained to perform particular kinds of services. The worldwide, multibillion-dollar industry has mushroomed beyond predictions. So there's a real shortage of competent people to staff it. Very few schools have caught up with the need to offer career-aimed courses. A handful of institutions turn out full-fledged motorcycle mechanics. One of these, on the West Coast, is known to have a huge waiting list. Applicants may be delayed as long as two years getting in.

Many positions call for individuals who have studied cycling from A to Z. Sales people, parts and accessories specialists, and service managers are among those needed to keep the millions of riders rolling.

All at once, there's a demand for real professionals to manage the critical aspects of cycling's terrific growth. Driver education teachers are on the "help wanted" list, if they can handle two-wheeled instruction. More and more traffic, licensing, and insurance agencies are hiring folks who know bikes.

Growing too are jobs for skilled riders. Police in several major cities are recruiting additional, cycle-mounted patrolmen. Bike-

Highly trained motorcycle mechanics are in short supply in many areas due to the accelerated growth of the sport and industry. Career opportunities have gone far ahead of schooling available for technicians. *Bernhard A. Roth Photo.*

Accessories, parts, and service are all included in the cycle rider and dealer relationship. Jobs for trained mechanics, parts managers, and salesmen are plentiful throughout the cycle industry. *Ed. De Rienze Photo.*

Motorcycles are in use by police forces all over the world. This is one of several specially equipped Triumph Thunderbirds that the Lancashire police (in England) are using to control high-speed traffic. *Arthur Winter Photo.*

riding messengers to deliver blueprints, advertising copy, and typographic materials are in lively demand to speed urgent items through traffic. Motorcycle factories employ a limited number of test riders who, generally, also qualify as mechanical engineers.

Each year a few more berths open among professional race riders. The boom in spectator interest encourages race promoters to lengthen calendars of events, including "spectaculars" held at huge indoor arenas. This means more money for more "lead shoes"—a thought for the talented fellow or girl with fierce competitive instincts.

Jobs featuring incidental cycle interest are also multiplying.

Two-wheeled adaptability for the press is used to cover a bicycle race in France. *BMW Photo.*

Cycles and scooters are often used to zip employees around big factories, warehouses, and supply yards. Greenskeepers use them to supervise golf course maintenance.

In the western United States, as well as in Australia and New Zealand, there's stepped-up usage of trail bikes to "punch" cattle and sheep. Dirt machines are on the upswing with conservation, park, forest, and wildlife officers as ideal means of tending to their far-flung duties.

Salaries in cycle vocations are as good as or better than those in comparable industries. The general rule, as elsewhere, is that the more you have invested in trade schooling or college education, plus experience, the larger will be your paycheck.

For further information, get in touch with such sources as your cycle dealer, educational guidance counselor, state department of public instruction, and personnel managers of the various motorcycle factories or sales organizations.

Contest Riders

Motorcycling surpasses other sports in the amount of intense, competitive activity packed into season after season. Any month at the height of riding weather, there are at least a thousand amateur contest-meets in action clear across the United States. In addition, there'll be a hundred or more professional programs under way—plus a dozen or so national championships up for grabs. This accounts only for activities officially sanctioned by the American Motorcycle Association (AMA). Informal rallies, tours, and field meets staged by hundreds of clubs add many other opportunities for cyclists to test skills and machines in a friendly atmosphere.

The American Motorcycle Association conducts about 95 percent of the organized cycle sport activities that take place in the United States. There are over 2,000 affiliated clubs currently staging more than 5,000 amateur events per year, with some 165,-000 rider entries.

For professional riders, recent years have averaged well over 400 regional events annually, and 25 national meets. Professionals must take out a competition license and pass an annual physical examination to continue racing. All start as novices and advance

A rider of a lightweight Japanese import—the Hodaka 100 BT—practices his motocross technique, an event that calls for frequent aerial acrobatics. *Hodaka Photo.*

to junior—to expert—only if they finish well in sufficient events. A goodly number of pros never make it to the expert class.

For more than a half century, AMA has held to its stated aims: "to foster strong and fair competition, to provide reasonable rules for the various types of competition, to administer the competition program with impartiality, and to reduce the hazards associated with the sport."

Regulations are aimed to protect the physical safety of riders and spectators alike. Great care is exercised to insure that all events are true contests among riders with machines having reasonably matching capabilities. Supervision of programs by AMA officials includes prompt dealing with violators and complaints, uniform design of competition courses, and a national system of ranking competitive riders.

Competitors are generally classed as either amateurs, who compete for trophies; or as professionals, who compete for money and trophies. Subclassifications in both groups are expert, junior, or novice. Ratings are given in accord with the individual rider's experience plus success in collecting points as a contestant in various approved events.

Riders must prove themselves in the hot, dusty saddle before moving up the ladder. For example, the current AMA *Professional Competition Rulebook* says: "All applicants for a professional license must have a Class A or Expert rating in Amateur competition if from an AMA district which has a recognized Amateur classification, upon proof of 2 years active Amateur scrambler competition or upon recommendation of his AMA district office."

Equally under pressure to prove their mettle in competition are the motorcycles. In fact, most improvements built into the superb performance and reliability of today's mass-produced bikes were conceived in many a mad dash for the checkered flag. Engines, transmissions, suspensions, steering, braking, and rider comforts have developed steadily to take the punishment of dirt trails and scorching pavement.

Fascinating variety in racing models and their fittings for each type of contest and location—plus a vast galaxy of events—beckon the cycle-sport fan to a yearly pageant of human skill and mechanical excellence. Currently, AMA lists the following events for professional riders: dirt track; short track; speedway; tourist trophy (TT); road race; motocross; and hillclimb.

In addition to the above events, AMA rules cover the following events for amateurs: scrambles; cross-country race; hare and hound; hare scrambles; enduro; reliability run; road run; poker run; ice race; drag race; economy run; observed field trials; plus dozens of other motorcycle games of particular interest to club riders.

MOTOCROSS . . . SOMETHING ELSE!

Probably no other cycle event uses up more excitement-stirred adrenalin in riders and spectators alike than does this European specialty. Introduced to the United States but a few years ago, motocross has zoomed to popularity from coast to coast. One reason is that a day of moto-X is often one of hours-long suspense, with the outcome in the balance all the way.

The course is as rough, rugged, and obstacle-riddled as can be found, within reasonable limits of safety. There are twists, turns, hairpins, nose dives, climbs, dipsy-doodles and jumps, and narrow lemon-squeezers. It's a closed circuit at least one-half mile in length.

Riders may be divided into nine classes according to engine size, beginning at the 100cc-and-under group, all the way up to 750cc and over. Each rider must swarm around the half-mile-plus circuit in each of three main heats for his class. Each heat runs a certain length of time. Winners are those having done the greatest number of laps when time is called. Points are awarded in order of finish position. For instance, four hundred points go to the first finisher— but just one point for the twentieth-place finisher. The over-all winner for each class, then, is the rider with the biggest total score.

By the hundreds and thousands, fans flock to witness feats of scenery juggling that a motorcycle can do better than any other vehicle on earth. Plunging down sheer embankments . . . leaping into space . . . skittering through brush like a scared jackrabbit. That's motocross.

Speeds are respectable, but the real object is pitting of rider skills. The ability to handle sand, gravel, and greasy clay . . . to hit the brake at just the right split second . . . knowing just which gears to pop, downslope and upslope.

"World series" in motocross are being staged currently at a dozen sites spanning the United States. Contests in the 500cc class

The lead shoe technique of cornering is used by a Sunday afternoon scrambles enthusiast at a club event in Pennsylvania. *Ed. De Rienze Photo.*

have been matching top European and American riders. Seasoned veterans from Czechoslovakia, Sweden, England, Belgium, and West Germany tend to ride off with the laurels. With experience, more Americans are inching into the winner's circle.

Each year, the event draws a bigger following. Better accommodations for the crowds are on the increase. For example, Ontario Speedway in Southern California built a motocross course inside its 2½-mile oval. Seating provides for 150,000 spectators.

WANNA SCRAMBLE?

The great popularity of this type of "go" is readily understood. For one thing, it brings out the best of the mechanical-cowboy tendencies that most of us have. For another, scrambling is designed especially for the nonprofessional rider; this takes in the bulk of the two-wheeled population. Simply stated, there are two kinds of competition; and these are directly related to the nature of the course.

Amateur scrambles (usually listed as just plain scrambles) take place on rough obstacle courses over natural terrain, such as pas-

"It happens every Sunday" isn't just the name of a movie about motorcycling. Here's a typical amateur's scramble scene—one of thousands of such events that take place weekly throughout the good-weather season. *Ed. De Rienze Photo.*

tures and woodland. The amount of course preparation will depend on the ambition and intent of local sponsors. But there'll be plenty of twisting and turning, and likely some hills and jumps.

TT scrambles, however, occur on better-prepared locations. Plenty of left- and right-hand turns, up- and downhill, keep things interesting. At least one jump will provide all contestants a chance to make like a bird. Because the underfooting, although dirt, is especially well-prepared, the TT gets to be mighty fast at the straights and turns.

All scrambles are closed-course, with no prescribed length of circuit. So many laps make a race. The object is strictly to beat the other guy to the checkered flag. Machines are laboriously fitted to answer the precise conditions of each course.

TASTE FOR TRACK

Shades of ye olde county fair! Holiday atmosphere . . . tense spectators in the bulging grandstand . . . dust devils out on the oval . . . the carnival spirit lives on in modern dirt track cycle

The flat track's fiercely competitive atmosphere is almost universally left to professional riders and ultratuned machinery. Shown is a field of novice class hot-shoes at Springfield, Illinois, in one of the nation's classic contests. *American Motorcycle Association Photo.*

racing. In fact, this kind of competition is often the climax event where fairs of local or state nature are still held. Promoters have found that they frequently draw larger crowds than any other kind of speed contest. The track layout is usually fairgrounds style, oval or egg-shaped. The terrain is commonly flat, although some sites do have banked turns. Track lengths are in three general categories: one mile; one-half mile; and less than one-quarter mile. The latter is usually referred to and listed as short track.

These events are just about 100 percent for professionals only. The pace is terrific. Riders must be razor-sharp. Refined maneuvers such as broad-sliding and other tricks of dirt-surface operation require long hours of practice. Machines are ultratuned and fitted to the calibration of a gnat's eyebrow.

So here's the place to watch or take part in wheel-to-wheel duels in the dust, sometimes inches from the barricades. If you want to attend a classic, note that they're often sold out months ahead!

HILLS ARE FOR CLIMBING

Here's one of cycling's greatest crowd-pleasers—guaranteed to drag even the nonriders away from their hot TV sets. Cycles and riders show they can give mountain goats a lesson or two in conquering nigh-impossible inclines. There are two general types of competition (providing we skip over the fussier details). The breakdown is between amateur and professional events.

Contests for amateurs attract the road rider who wants to demonstrate his bike's talents at performing on its hind leg. The machine may have little or no special preparation; it may have just street tires. The amateur event may run against the clock, or two bikes at a time, in drag style.

Professional climbers, on the other hand, go all-out to prepare their bikes. Weight reduction, special forks, sprockets, tire treads, and chains come into play. So do special fuel mixes and highly refined carburetor adjustments. Changes in air humidity may throw them out of tune. Pro events run strictly against the clock.

The main object in any case is to get up across that finish line without somersaulting, sunfishing, etc.—in quickest fashion. Some slopes are fifty degrees—darned close to straight up!

RUGGED ENDUROS AND TRIALS

Need proof that a motorcycle is about the toughest, most versatile hunk of machinery in the world? . . . Or that the ace riders are likewise? . . . Then get yourself to an enduro, or give one a try. The events are not especially designed for spectators, since they're strung out anywhere up to five hundred miles in length. However, onlookers do sometimes crawl for hours through the bushes just to see some spectacular section, such as a water crossing or a bog.

All sorts of hazards are thrown at the enduro rider: fallen logs, boulders, sand, and mud; mountains one moment and oozy ditchbanks the next. They call for all known skills in riding, plus the last-it-out will of a bulldog. For what? Usually, just a crazy but cherished trophy like an old cowbell, or a chance to tell your grandchildren you made it to the finish line. Two out of three often fall

The trials competition is among the more rugged cycle events, testing the rider's ability to cope with nigh-impossible terrain without putting a foot down in transit. *Montesa Photo.*

by the wayside, as in the classic Jack Pine Enduro held annually at Lansing, Michigan.

Navigating ability is just as important to stay on route and maintain the correct arrival time at various checkpoints. Points are deducted for being early, late, or for similar boo-boos. In Europe, trials are much the same kind of event. Most famous is the

John Giles, the longest-serving member of the Triumph works team, seen participating in the International Six-Day Trials in Czechoslovakia on a Triumph 500cc machine. *Triumph Photo.*

International Six-Day Trials—a yearly team contest interrupted only by wars over a span of half a century. Enduro and trial machines are rigged to face every condition met on land or sea.

INSIDE ROAD-RACING

Blinding speeds . . . the roar of sharply tuned engines . . . mounting suspense . . . the color of large crowds and numerous contestants . . . these are some of the elements that make road races unique in cycling sport. These are the longest races, climaxing in the two-hundred-mile National Championship classic held annually at Daytona Beach, Florida. Although there are subclassifications related to the types of cycles, the two general rider-groups are amateur and professional. As with other events, amateur races award trophies only. Professionals compete for cash prizes and trophies.

A Harley-Davidson Streamliner with Cal Rayborn shoehorned into the cockpit prepares for a record-breaking run at the world-famed Bonneville Salt Flats in Utah. The Sportster engine-powered bomb averaged 265.492 mph, a new top. *Harley-Davidson Photo.*

Cal Rayborn smiles understandably on completion of his run at the Bonneville Salt Flats. The pneumatic skids at the rear end held the sportster-power streak upright in the initial stage in the dash for supremacy as the world's fastest motorcycle. *Harley-Davidson Photo.*

Road racing attracts the nation's most highly competitive, skilled riders. Machines are tuned to the perfection of musical instruments. Great care is given to suspension, carburetion, ignition systems, tires, fueling—in fact, to every tiny or large component of the racing bike. Streamlining becomes critical. So does the size of fuel tank, when pit stops may be involved.

Courses are paved. Plentiful left- and right-hand turns and "S's" combined with embankments, simulate conditions a rider might meet in racing over the countryside, through village and town. The length of lap varies according to each track. Straightaways enable spectacular acceleration—approaching 200 mph for the big bikes at some of the classic locations.

RACING SPEEDS

In short-track (quarter-mile) events, professionals of all classes use 250cc machines topping at about 65 mph. On half-mile and mile dirt tracks, juniors and experts are allowed to run 750cc machinery; on mile track straights they hit up to 120 mph.

During AMA (paved) road races, professional riders use either 250cc or 750cc bikes. Depending on the track, the 250s may reach 135 mph, and the 750s around 160 mph.

Amateurs on large-displacement cycles have been known to register 80 mph crossing wide-open spaces often used for western hare-and-hound racing.

A Place for Us

Special parks and reservations where fellows, girls, and whole families can get together and ride motorcycles, minis, and scooters to their hearts' content—this is a brand-new idea beginning to catch fire around the United States.

There are about a hundred such areas at present. More are in the planning or serious talk stages. Some now operating provide four hundred to five hundred acres or more terrain for fun riding of all sorts. This includes gentle, woodsy trails and fields for novices and youngsters; also rugged slopes, tricky sand washes, and water crossings for those who prefer rough going.

The really big advantage is that two-wheeled folks can be by themselves. They can share lively activities and exchange useful knowledge without worrying about interference. Designated places like these are becoming more important daily.

GRAB FOR SPACE

You don't need a crystal ball to see that America is in the "more everything" era. Every day you can notice that there's more *something* than the day before: more houses, office buildings, roads, shopping centers, schools, and, certainly, more people. Since nearly everyone becomes a motor vehicle operator, we have a skyrocketing

Environmental awareness is growing strong among all users of the outdoors—
including cyclists. *RVI Photo.*

number of autos, trucks, trailer-campers, motor homes, snowmobiles, and—fortunately—motorcycles.

All these items—new construction, the rubber-tired brigade, and
people—claim their share of space. Problems begin with the fact
that dry land surface space, or elbow room in which to do our thing,
can't be stretched. The two billion acres of the United States are
likely to be *all we'll ever have.* As the saying goes, "Everyone's got

to be *some*place." So the squeeze is on. This kind of pressure has already affected motorcycling in many crowded city areas.

The bike is essentially at its best in wide-open spaces, where nimble wheels are free to roam. Handy in normal traffic it surely is as well. But it's no particular pleasure to ride amid solid phalanxes of cars, trucks, and buses, creeping at snail's pace, and smothered in the exhaust of four-wheeled commuters. As a result, increasing numbers of cyclists have "taken to the hills," or are making the attempt. Their ambition is to leave crowds behind and find new freedom in spacious back country.

Difficulties arise in the eastern United States. There, most land is privately owned, and land owners don't always welcome bikes with open arms. Better chances for open-space riding occur west of the Mississippi River, where the federal government owns huge parcels of public land in seventeen western states. Yet, even on public land, East or West, there are conflicts in land use among motorcyclists, other outdoorsmen, and the public at large. Differences need to be straightened out now and in years ahead.

CYCLE CRITICS

Anyone active in the sport should know that motorcycling has opponents and what causes this opposition. Bear in mind only about one out of a dozen households owns a bike. Millions of people, therefore, have no idea of riding pleasures. They have no motive to care whether the cyclist's rightful needs are met. All the more reason for two-wheelsmen to listen carefully to critics, and to respond in a common-sense way.

Many types of off-road vehicles—Jeeps, snowmobiles, ATVs, and dune buggies—are accused of hurting the natural environment. The cycle is sometimes singled out as a special target. "Too much noise" is a criticism thought justified enough to call for forthright action on the part of the United States' billion-dollar-a-year motorcycle industry.

Several companies are busy developing new types of mufflers and accessories that take the "bark and scream" out of two- and four-stroke engines. Indications are that all pleasure bikes will soon produce minimum sounds only. Similar action is under way in mo-

The two-wheeler's extreme maneuverability, on or off the road, helps account for its unique popularity. *Bernhard A. Roth Photo.*

torcycle racing machinery. Competition's chief governing body, the American Motorcycle Association, has moved swiftly to require muffling in all sanctioned enduros and hare-and-hound events.

In addition, AMA has decreed muffling for all amateur events, and for all professional motocross contests. Sponsoring clubs are responsible for measuring sounds of competing machines to insure compliance with antinoise rules. Signs point toward reasonably quiet motorcycling and fewer complaints from hikers, naturalists, and others who want tranquillity in the wilderness.

Devices that prevent hot sparks from spewing out of exhaust pipes have been used by off-road vehicles for a number of years. These so-called "spark arresters" are customarily installed on trail bikes. Designs that meet fire-preventing standards set by the U. S. Forest Service are enforced in national forests and parks and other public grounds. That vehicles of all types are capable of tearing up virgin soil and useful vegetation is another point often made by environmental conservationists.

Motorcycledom is responding to this challenge. Information supplied through trail clubs, magazines, and advertisements of the Motorcycle Industry Council (MIC) is sharpening riders' alertness to avoiding this kind of resource damage. Courses laid out for cross-country events, such as enduros, are being deliberately altered to eliminate possible injury to valuable plant species, wildlife, and water sources.

Examples reveal that much is being done to make motorcycling ever more in harmony with the outdoor heritage. As the bike grows in popularity and more people understand the machine, added areas may be unlocked for rider enjoyment. In densely populated sections, areas for motorcycles only may be the best answer for off-road yearnings of many riders.

MOTORCYCLE PRESERVES

You may want to take a hand in supporting some type of public cycling setup for your community. If you're seriously interested, there are helpful information and details available from the Motorcycle Industry Council and the U. S. Bureau of Outdoor Recreation. Both offices are located in Washington, D.C.

In an MIC booklet on motorcycle parks, magazine editor Chuck Clayton wrote: "All of the facilities and conditions for motorcycle recreation are capable of being accommodated in state, municipal and county parks, provided there is sufficient space and suitable terrain not committed to other park uses. Other public lands under jurisdiction of public utilities, flood control land and lands reserved for sanitary fills would also be suitable for limited periods of motorcycle use.

"Land for a motorcycle recreation reserve should not be expensive. Often the very characteristics which lower real estate value (irregular surface, large hills, steepness, high water table) make it *more* valuable to the sporting rider. Much land which does not readily adapt itself to other uses and is available at low cost, can be made productive by its dedication to motorcycle recreation."

Since cycle preserves are still few in number, there aren't many people who know what they're like. Reports indicate that successful ones now operating have a great deal to offer.

Outstanding features are good access roads and ample parking,

The European-style motocross is highly popular at a growing number of new motorcycle preserves being established to insure legal off-road riding. This is part of a field of three hundred riders at Indian Dunes Park, California. *Dwight Vaccaro Photo.*

so that riders may ride or trailer in and out in safety and convenience. Many areas have facilities for relaxed picnicking and outdoor cooking in scenic comfort. Variety in riding terrain is furnished to satisfy all levels of rider competence, including protected space for learners and young fry exercising their minis.

Traffic controls are observed, such as one-way systems on tracks and trails to avoid accidents. Provision is made to eject any riders who refuse to cooperate for the good of the group. Excellent riding habits are established, including the use of protective clothing, helmets, and insuring proper mechanical condition of bikes admitted.

Reserves operated commercially charge a modest fee of a few dollars for a day's dawn-to-dusk riding privileges. Some reserves stage regular races, motocross, and scrambles, including events for juniors, that add spice to family outings. From all accounts, it

Ahead lies a rough road, but the adventuring cyclist is confident that he and his two-wheeled steed will make it through. *Bernhard A. Roth Photo.*

seems that motorcycle parks have a bright future in offering badly needed off-highway riding space in many parts of the country.

"WINGS" ON YOUR WHEELS

A prediction: The day you discover that your chosen vehicle is *not* hog-tied to surfaces made of concrete, asphalt, crushed rock— or man-built roads of any sort—will be a thrill like signing your own declaration of independence. Just how you'll embark upon this added world of riding pleasure may occur in one of many ways. Perhaps you'll swing off a sun-baked highway, seeking cool shade . . . and just keep right on going, deeper and deeper into the inviting forest.

Or maybe an unfamiliar roadway will unexpectedly end and some voice inside you whisper, "Don't stop now. Go and go and go." You can't resist, so you plunge into the realm of untried grass, brush, swampy swales, and sandy hummocks. Your mount responds eagerly to the challenge.

It could be that a dirt-enthusiastic friend will flaunt his tailpipe

Just rambling through the woods and fields in the back country is tops for fun and adventure. *Bernhard A. Roth Photo.*

in your face as he dives into the nearest thicket. You'll be doggoned if he can stump you; so you dive after him, and stick to him like a burr. The merry ramble takes you far from the pavements of ordinary motorists, to a thousand fresh sensations never known in four-wheeled confinement.

For now, you've become brother to the sprinting jackrabbit, bounding deer, and steel-spring-legged mountain goat. From now on, you'll seek to match their speed and agility in terrain that nature alone made. You and your bike have found a deeper respect for each other and new rules to go by, in the off-road way of life.

TRAIL A BIKE

Some automobiles are bad news for would-be users of bumper racks. We have found American-made models whose bumpers are fitted so snugly that a bike can't be racked without special rigging. Extensions have to be made in a machine shop.

Recently we discovered a foreign-make sedan that raised still a

A permanent-type trailer hitch is bolted to the car chassis. The rack for the bike's wheel is bolted to the hitch. The holding chains can be made extremely tight and hold the cycle secure. *Bernhard A. Roth Photo.*

A good rig for trailing a bike behind a car. The main weight of the machine rests on the rear wheel. *Bernhard A. Roth Photo.*

different problem. The bumper twisted alarmingly like aluminum foil when we racked a two-hundred-pound dirt cruiser on it. This brought on visions of our six-hundred-dollar love doing painful handsprings on the thruway in back of us while we buzzed off, all unaware of the happening.

We checked an unbelievable number of people and finally, at a remote dealership, found a gadget to solve the problem. Required is a permanent-type trailer hitch, bolted securely to the car chassis. A beefy single rack that swallows the bike's front wheel is then bolted to the trailer hitch. Next, a heavy link chain is fastened, running from the front fork clamp and hooking onto one of the bumper brackets. A second chain is attached from the fork clamp to the other bracket. By compressing the fork and heeling the bike over, both chains can be made as taut as bowstrings. The main weight of the machine rests on the free, rear wheel.

With this method, a bike may be towed at reasonably high speeds—best 5 to 10 mph *below* the maximum. Moderate speed around sharp turns is recommended to avoid a tail-wagging effect and possible damage. Gradual rather than violent braking will take possible strain off the fork.

On a long jaunt, remove the master link and flip the chain off the rear sprocket. Wire the chain to the frame out of harm's way. This is a precaution against a jounce accidentally popping the transmission into gear. Damage to the engine and other parts could be severe.

Backing up a car with a trailed bike is very difficult. It's a lot easier to get headed in the right direction—and then attach the motorcycle. Otherwise, have an assistant guide the bike by truing it up at intervals, while the driver backs up slowly and easily. Most toll roads tack on the rate of a single-wheeled trailer when a machine is tugged along in this fashion.

Family Fun Awheel

A good place to examine the new movement toward specially dedicated space for motor sports is at Indian Dunes Park, thirty-seven miles north of Los Angeles on the Golden State Freeway. You'll learn that this was the first off-road family motor recreation park in Los Angeles County—and among the first of its type in the nation.

Sprawled across six hundred acres of mountain, mesa, and river bottom are complete facilities for minibikes, motorcycles, dune buggies, micromidgets, and four-wheel-drive vehicles. For safety, each kind of vehicle has its assigned area. The varied terrain affords hill-climbing and a sand racing basin with a running stream to ford. Picnic areas are reserved under cottonwood trees where families can keep an eye on the special minibike corral for young children.

Every day in the week, from morning until night, Indian Dunes enthusiasts may tackle twenty miles of scenic, tree-lined trails; a genuine international motocross obstacle course; less demanding courses for beginners and families; and a one-sixth-mile oval dirt track. A day's admission ranges from two dollars for two-wheelers up to five dollars for four-wheelers, with special rates for groups and clubs. Spectators are encouraged with a special lower rate per carful.

John Grout of the park management says: "We've opened our new Shadow Glen motocross. Designed in the true European fashion—tight and twisty—it winds through a picture-book area of large shade trees and gently rolling hills. We conduct motocross racing every Sunday, with a ride attendance of more than three hundred for every program. Also on the racing schedule—usually twice a month—is an all-junior motocross program, which helps to provide a start for the beginning rider in special divisions of their own."

The problem of where to go is being partially answered by Indian Dunes Park and others developing across the country. Their special value is the *legal* opportunity for off-road riding, family style. They also relieve the growing scarcity of sites vitally needed to conduct professional racing—and train young riders in razor-sharp skills essential for competition.

HOW'S OUR "E.Q."?

Those letters stand for "environmental quality," a big issue in the United States today. Fish and wildlife are dying in streams

Designated riding parks and preserves are often the only safe and sane outlets for very young riders with their various mini two-wheelers. *Yamaha Photo.*

fouled with spillover from dumps, industries, construction, and household wastes. The problem is everybody's, including motorcyclists. We, too, affect the natural environment.

Our engines pollute the air along with those of buses, jet planes, trucks, and trains; coal-burning, heat, and electric plants; and, of course, the millions of automobiles. The number of cycles, scooters and minibikes is, however, a drop in the bucket compared to other fuel-burners.

Also, the average two-wheeled motor is a midget compared to the power plant in an average automobile. For every 150cc-powered bike, there are many times more 150 *cubic inch*-powered automobiles. A cubic inch is 16.5 cubic centimeters. That means that each auto, in this example, has the capacity to spew out some fifteen times larger amounts of exhaust.

New laws are requiring all manufacturers to install devices that cut down obnoxious exhaust. Motorcycle engines must also comply. Cycle firms have also agreed to reduce motor noise.

Peace and quiet are among the top values sought by most hikers, canoeists, mountain climbers, and fishermen. Motorcycle, snowmobile, and ATV enthusiasts simply must learn to adapt to and respect the desires of other, more silent outdoorsmen. Adjustments are being made and will continue, by regulation and improved mutual understanding.

Two-wheeled sportsmen have a good record in relieving one of the nation's most vexing pollution problems. The trouble is that of crowding. A fancier term might be "open space pollution." Examples are snarled lines of motor traffic and plugged-up parking areas.

The motorcyclist seldom uses more than about 20 square feet of the road; the autoist uses at least 140 square feet. To demonstrate this point, bike folks in several cities have held "parking rallies": They showed police that the usual metered slot will hold 4 to 6 cycles, in place of a single passenger car. They weren't trying to "put down" regular motorists; the point was that motorcyclists deserve equal consideration from officials who write vehicle laws and set up parking facilities.

Before taking your two-wheeler into a state or national park it is a good idea to check on the regulations. *Bernhard A. Roth Photo.*

An interesting fact brought to light was that, in commuter traffic, autos and cycles each rarely carried more than a single passenger/operator. In pollution control and efficient use of space and fuel resources, therefore, higher marks went to the bike. Used properly, the motorcycle shows promise as a vehicle favoring a high-quality environment.

The Sound of Motor Music

For years, motor sportsmen generally thought that their beloved engines just *had* to produce unearthly noises. The more deafening the racket, the better were chances for speed—so they believed. Lately the public has spoken out, demanding relief from unnecessary ear-beating all over the land. Stiff sound-pollution laws have been enacted. Construction companies, factories, airlines, and now the motorcycle industry are being pressed to "muzzle" their noises down to reasonable limits.

Meanwhile, a happy discovery has come to light: Tests made with newly designed mufflers indicate that these devices can actually improve motorcycle engine horsepower and torque. *Also, such improvements occur at highest revolutions per minute: the RPMs that usually create the biggest noise.*

Experiments directed by the American Motorcycle Association clearly showed that bikes don't have to be ear-splitters in order to deliver performance. AMA used a 100cc Hodaka as a pilot model, gunning it to 9,000 RPMs in metering three different muffler installations. A conventional street-type muffler gave off a reasonable 86 decibels of sound. An open expansion chamber pipe caused a screaming 97 db reading. But a new, muffled expansion chamber unit cut the racket back down to 86 db's.

A removable baffle on an H-D Shortster minibike permits the installation of a silencer and spark arrester. *Bernhard A. Roth Photo.*

Further, the brand-new muffler design resulted in 12 horsepower and 23 foot-pounds of torque, a *bonus* of 3.5 hp and 6.5 ft-lbs of torque *more* than the mind-blowing, unmuffled expansion chamber delivered at peak revs. "Comparable results are being achieved with most models for which a silenced expansion chamber is being produced," says the organization's official journal, AMA *News*.

The modern-breed exhaust silencer does two jobs for the cycle engine. Most designs provide a chamber that tunes the flowage and pressure of exhaust gases in a manner to encourage horsepower and torque. To this is added the silencer unit. This consists of a length of perforated pipe wrapped in glass fiber: The material has far greater sound-absorbing efficiency than the series of sound baffles installed in older units.

Silencer-adapters that can be welded to unimproved chambers are being marketed. Good advice is to check carefully that such units will produce hoped-for results. Also, be certain the rig will pass state inspections before rushing out a mail order for one.

The unit for measuring sound, the *decibel,* is news to many people. The abbreviation is db, and a complete account of its meaning could go on for many pages. There are, for instance, numerous ways to take a db reading with sound-level metering devices. In one method applied to motorcycles, the reading is taken from a position 50 feet to the rear, with the machine standing still. Still another system is to read the meter as a bike moves past at 35 mph.

A key thing to note is that even a minor increase in the decibel reading can mean a fantastic increase in the intensity of the sound being measured. Take an alarm clock ring rated at 80 db. Compare it with an 85 db-rated roar of rush-hour traffic in a large city: Only 5 more db's, but a terrific gain in volume of sound. Sound technologists describe 120 db's as the "threshold of pain," the point where most people become ill or violently upset. Lesser intensities annoy many.

The throaty gurgle, mutter, thrumming—whatever you want to call it—of a healthy engine turning over is music to many a motorcyclist. No one is trying to enforce total silence, really. But if the sport is to continue flourishing, the warning flags are up. "Piping down" in good neighborly fashion is the only choice we have.

Chopper's Choice

A word about a wholly different subcontinent in the world of motorcycling. Rarely does the complete beginner become immediately concerned with the rigorous art of chopping bikes. It is "rigorous" in terms of the money, time, and talent required for success. Fascination it surely possesses, as many a garish poster, sensational movie, and record-album cover will bear out.

The term "chop" originates with owner tendencies to chop off, shorten, or reduce the bike's stock components to achieve his tastes in restyling. Bobtailed fenders and stubby pipes are examples in point. It would be unfair to "put down" all choppers in a flat statement of dismissal. Chop jobs should be judged on their individual merits. Many are simply expressions of the individuality that nearly all cyclists cherish—granted that some go to "outasight" extremes.

Under skilled hands, a radically chopped or custom-styled bike can indeed be a thing of beauty in glittering chrome, blazoning color, and sculptured configuration. And when the owner can step back, look at his handiwork, and say, "That is *me*, the way I like it!"—to him, it is mission accomplished.

Chopper fans' interests move in three general directions: "show"; "go"; and "show and go." The terms pretty well speak for

Custom painting, bobbed fenders and tail pipes, extended springer forks, lightweight front wheel, king and queen saddle, square handlebars, etc., add a thousand dollars to the investment in an H-D sportster. It is pretty, but unsafe and not "street legal" as seen here. *Ed. De Rienze Photo.*

themselves. Many in the first group mentioned ride their glistening creations scarcely more than on and off the trailer heading for the nearest motorcycle exposition. The "go" group are hot for performance plus modified styling. The "show and go" crowd aims for a balance between elegance and roadability.

It is with the "monkey see, monkey do" type of chopping—alterations that ruin perfectly good machinery—that veteran riders, seasoned designers, and dealers throw up their hands in horror; especially when the result is a monstrosity that is both unsafe and illegal to run on a public road.

Chopping or way-out customizing, however successful, has built-in risks. Its individuality is valued only by its owner. This means that he will seldom be able to reclaim all the money and effort he has put into it. For instance, we recently viewed a brand-new superbike, freshly chopped to the tune of at least a thousand dollars. The retail price of the bike was two thousand dollars. It would be highly unlikely to go on resale for more than twelve hundred dollars, as against the three thousand sunk in the machine.

The moral seems to be: Chop if you must, but go into it with a well-conceived design and your eyes wide open to what you're getting into. Meanwhile, most authorities agree that numerous ideas from the chopper's art—in paint and accessory trimming, in comfort and eye appeal—have enhanced modern motorcycling.

Accessory Tips

Thousands of items crowd cycle mail-order catalogs and dealer shelves. Well-selected accessories add performance, fun, and comfort. Others glitter—and that's about all they do. Assuming you have basic equipment—helmet; goggles; riding apparel, including boots and gloves—what else is really useful?

The best advice of veteran motorcyclists is this: Buy extras, bit by bit, as you experience the *need*. Set your own priorities according to the kind of riding you do most. Following are some ideas and approximate costs. Choice will depend on whether you're a trailster, commuter, or tourist—or all three and then some.

Bungee cords. Carry a couple at all times, to secure bundles, bags, packages—also for emergencies like holding on a loose tail-pipe, battery cover, etc. $.75 to $2.50.

Luggage rack. Capacity to tote things is handy for nearly any kind of ride. $10 to $20.

Hand rail. Extra safety for the passenger—also a convenient point to attach bedroll, knapsack, etc. $12 and up.

Reflectors. You probably have the minimum required by state inspection. Install a few more along your flanks. Some dark night they could save your life. $.75 to $1.50 apiece.

Saddlebags. For ordinary flitting about, these provide much

The well-dressed cyclist ready to go riding. *Ed. De Rienze Photo.*

more space than needed. Their real purpose is major haulage. $30 to $70 a pair.

Safari case. Or some such name. A simple box with a lid that can be locked. A useful size will hold a couple of helmets and a hearty picnic. $20 to $40.

A level stretch of road or beach is a good choice for beginners to learn basic handling and what their machine can do. This rider is well protected with boots, helmet, goggles, and gloves. *Yamaha Photo.*

Saddles. Be kind to that part of you that gets the most wear and tear. *Solo*, a new experience, $30 to $50. *Super-buddy*, change your seating for less fatigue, in the $65 range.

Tool case. Why all bikes don't come equipped with this, we'll never know. Up to $18.

Center stand. Ideal for oil changes, lubricating, and other maintenance. $15 to $20.

Engine guard. Sometimes called a skid plate. For riders of the "badlands." Once you've seen a punctured transmission, you're sold. $25 to $35.

Bumper brackets. To portage the bike weighing up to 300 pounds. In the $35 range.

Spark arrester. Without one on many public lands, you'll get hauled in. Up to $25.

Extra foot pegs. Put a second set in a position that will enable uncramping your legs on a long highway jaunt. Allow for $10 a pair.

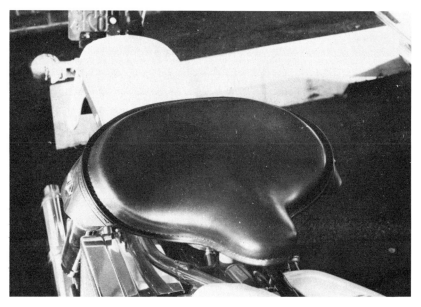

A solo saddle offers a more secure seat for the single operator/passenger. *Bernhard A. Roth Photo.*

A frame-mounted buddy seat on a motorcycle with Fiberglas saddle bags, guard rails, hand rail, and luggage rack. *Bernhard A. Roth Photo.*

Tuned expansion chambers. Be ready for environmental law enforcement. Noise cutters may cost $40 or more.

Service manual. Or "shop manual." Far more descriptive than your rider manual. Tells exactly how your bike goes together and comes apart, down to the last nut, bolt, and washer. Loads of pictures and diagrams. A good investment. Can cost $8 to $10, and save you that much on a single problem.

Turn signals. Best designs are "self-canceling"—that is, they quit blinking when you straighten out from a turn. Otherwise, be sure yours has a clear signal (buzzer, dashlight, etc.) that tells you what the blinkers are doing. In Pennsylvania, where we live, blinkers are not required. However, when used, they must be positioned 36 inches apart for legal standing in a court case resulting from an accident. $36 to $45 a set.

Windshield. A wide choice from simple wind-breakers to rather complete protection, including streamlined fairings. $18 to $60.

License plate brackets. For some reason, manufacturers don't realize that plates get curled, dog-eared, and plain beat-up without reinforced mounting. Around $1 or $1.50.

Lock-up devices. Case-hardened chains, padlocks, cables, what-have-you. They're worth the price in these sticky-fingered times. Could easily repay $10 or so outlay.

Special mounting for major accessories, such as saddles, may run the bill upward considerably. Some dealers may add installation labor costs. Get the whole story before giving the go-ahead.

WINDSHIELD SURVEY

Many riders turn "thumbs down" on windshields. Some just prefer the primitive feel of unchecked air beating on their faces and bodies. And it truly is a "flying" sensation like piloting one of the old open-cockpit airplanes. Other objectors to shields claim that the gadgets spoil visibility and slow them down, because of air resistance. There's something to both these opinions.

A dirty, discolored shield definitely obstructs vision, and, at night, it picks up headlight glare to a hazardous degree. If a bike has plenty of power, the air resistance will hardly be noticed.

For dirt riding through brush and woodsy terrain, a shield is

A flared windshield with a slot cut at eye level. This insures a clear spot to peer through at night and when dust and grime might obscure the remainder of the shield. *G. Smith Photo.*

another protrusion likely to get snagged by low-hanging twigs and branches. Face shields are a far better recommendation, off road.

Well-designed, securely mounted windshields do come into their own in several highly advantageous conditions. First of all, they offer a great deal more protection than meets the eye. They act to deflect vast quantities of road grit and airborne debris, including hordes of insects in the summertime. In motion, they create a moving pocket of still air in which the rider experiences less fatigue, especially on a long trip.

Some designs of streamlined type have fairings extending over the handlebar grips. On a chilly ride, the operator enjoys comparative warmth right down to his fingertips. Comes a sudden rain shower, and he rides remarkably high and dry. In all except the foulest weather, he travels along sheltered in his own private bubble.

A streamlined fairing may actually add a few additional miles per hour of speed for a given throttle setting. It simply offers better air penetration, like an airplane's cowlings and airfoils. For the enthusiast bent on a good deal of highway tripping and touring, the regular shield is worth investigating.

A good shield has qualities you will recognize. It will attach to your machine with minimum vibration. It won't conflict with hand-lever controls or installation of a rear-view mirror. And it will not cut off your view of turn-signal indicators, if you happen to have them. This latter point is worth checking.

The windshield should be set so that you can easily peer over the top of it. A type we recommend highly has a peekaboo slot sliced out at eye level. The beauty of this feature is an absolutely clear space to look through, no matter how fouled the shield may become.

Even a miniaturized shield may be appreciated on an hours-long ride. The effect is to divert excessive air pressures from the rider's person. There's no need to hang onto handlebars like grim death.

WIND FACTORS

You're spinning along the highway, just minding your own affairs as you watch the world come toward you. Suddenly you're drowned in raucous noise that spills over you from the rear. Shock waves seem to beat on your helmet. Your eyes flick wildly sidewise to see a huge diesel semivan go highballing past.

If you've been through a similar experience, you know what to expect. First comes a high-powered breaker of rolling air that tries to sweep you clean off the road and into a ditch. Next comes a rotary trail of turbulence gusting in several directions at the same time. It buffets you from all sides.

Your only defense is to tighten your knee-grip on the tank and clench the handlebar like grim death. Meanwhile, your reflexes help you do a balancing act like those high-wire artists in the circus. Unavoidably, you lean rapidly back and forth fighting for equilibrium until the air quiets down.

When it's *your* turn to pass a truck, there's still another hazard to remember. The fast-moving bulk creates a vacuum that can

Jackets of leather or other windproof material with zippered closures are standard wearing apparel for cycle riders. *Ed. De Rienze Photo.*

suck you and your bike into it. Be sure you've got ample power and speed to break away from that force before trying to pass.

Air currents, wind, and air resistance have considerable effect on motorcycle performance. For instance, there's no more pitiful sight than an overloaded, underpowered cycle holding up a line of fuming motorists, going uphill into a strong headwind. This example helps to explain why some expressway officials won't allow bikes below a certain horsepower rating—or reject them altogether.

Know therefore, for sure, what your little corn popper can really do against an oncoming breeze. A facing wind at 15 mph may cut your speed by half that velocity. And there you are, with no more throttle left to bail you out. This can be less than fun, with 200–300 hp four-wheeled speedsters all around you.

Air moving past your body either as wind, or as air brushed aside as you buzz through it, surely affects bodily comfort. On a moderate day, you find yourself getting extra thirsty as passing air draws moisture from your skin. On a cool day, your first sensation is likely to be that of feeling a *lot* cooler. Passing air swiftly subtracts body heat. In fact, a ride in near-freezing airs can give you almost unbelievable chills. The temperature you feel through an exposed point, such as your nose, is directly related to the speed you're gunning through the open air.

We recommend that you have a good look at the wind-chill table. It will give you scientific reasons for bundling up from head to toe when the frost is on the pumpkin.

WIND-CHILL EQUIVALENT TEMPERATURE
WIND VELOCITY (MPH)

Temp. F°	3	5	7	10	15	20	25	35	50
40	40	34	30	23	20	15	11	7	4
35	35	29	24	18	12	7	3	−2	−5
30	30	24	17	12	3	−1	−5	−13	−16
25	25	17	13	3	−4	−9	−15	−20	−24
20	20	12	7	−4	−13	−18	−23	−28	−33
15	15	5	−1	−11	−20	−24	−33	−37	−40
10	10	0	−7	−17	−27	−33	−38	−45	−50
0	0	−13	−18	−29	−40	−46	−53	−61	−58
−10	−10	−23	−31	−42	−53	−60	−68	−77	−65
−20	−20	−33	−43	−55	−67	−76	−85	−93	−75

To help you interpret this table in terms of motorcycling, here are a few examples.

For simplicity, let's use just two sets of figures: Take the line opposite the temperature reading of 30°, and the columns under wind velocity. With the wind speed at 0 mph, it can be seen that the chill effect is 30°, which is the same as the temperature reading.

Now let's assume you're riding the bike at 35 mph. Look at the line opposite the temperature, 30°. Under 35 mph, you'll see the chill effect is −13 degrees, or 13° below 0°.

Note that riding along at 35 mph on a still day is the same as *making* the wind blow 35 mph.

Now, if the wind begins to blow at 10 mph and you ride *into* it, you *add* that to the speed at which you're riding your bike. Thus if you're traveling at 40 mph, your body is exposed to a 50 mph (40 mph plus 10 mph) wind speed factor. Take a look in the chill effect opposite 30° and you'll see the effect is actually −16°.

Whenever the chill effect approaches 20° below 0°, you're risking frozen hands, feet, etc., if they're not protected. The wind-chill table is used regularly to insure proper cold-weather clothing and equipment for military personnel, construction workers, and others who operate outdoors constantly. This scientific information may keep you comfortable, too.

KEEPING WARM AND DRY

Thunderheads began to build up in the sky overhead as we rolled along through scenic farmland in southeastern Pennsylvania. Bam! Someone threw the switch and umpteen swollen clouds unloaded on us. We were soaked to the skin instantly.

After the first avalanche, the rain calmed to a steady drizzle. We kept on cruising. With only an hour and a half travel ahead of us, our aim was to brave it out. Inside of thirty minutes, we felt ice-cold, shivering so much we just had to do something. It was midday. At the first motel we sighted we explained our plight. The lady in charge rented us a room for two hours, wherein we dived into a hot shower. We turned a fan on our sodden clothes. After the treatment, we were able to survive the rest of the trip. It cost two bucks and was worth every nickel.

The lesson we learned is that a sopping wet rider moving at 50 mph is really a human refrigeration unit. The wind gets busy extracting the moisture, which in turn draws warmth from the body. Swiftly, a person becomes a human icicle—even on a warm summer day such as described above. The better makes of clothing designed especially for cyclists are water-*repellent*. They'll stand several hours of rain-beating before moisture begins to penetrate.

This amount of protection may be enough, unless prolonged foul weathering is expected. Then you might want to consider water-*proof* material in the plastic or rubberized fabric line. To be avoided is raingear that stiffens in the cold; has poor ventilation; and/or flaps like the rags on a scarecrow in a breeze. Watch also for poor closures that send dank drafts up pant legs, sleeves, and down the neck.

With any garment eyed for the cold or wet, be sure it offers bodily freedom before buying. As a case in point, we once bought a pair of Air Force surplus flying pants. Indeed they were wondrous warm. In quick succession we discovered: (1) They forced a seating position that brought on an agonizing cramp in our thigh region; (2) they were so bulky we could barely hike up our leg to kick the starter over. Good-bye flying pants.

In bundling against the cold, the first line of defense is outer material that breaks the wind. Inside you want to achieve the maximum amount of dead air spaces. Here is where your body heat stays put. You can buy pants and jackets—or suits—with air spaces built in. Or you can create air spaces by adding as many layers of undergarments as you find necessary. This may include "thermal" underwear.

There are custom cycle-suits on the market that are just the ticket. They're expensive but nice to have.

There are advantages in both approaches to fighting the cold. A single pants/jacket combo generally has less bulk and affords more body mobility. On the other hand, an extra shirt or a sweater can be more easily shucked off or put on, to fit sudden changes in temperature. Quilted drawers may offer a bit of a problem if the crowd decides to crouch near a hot stove somewhere along the route.

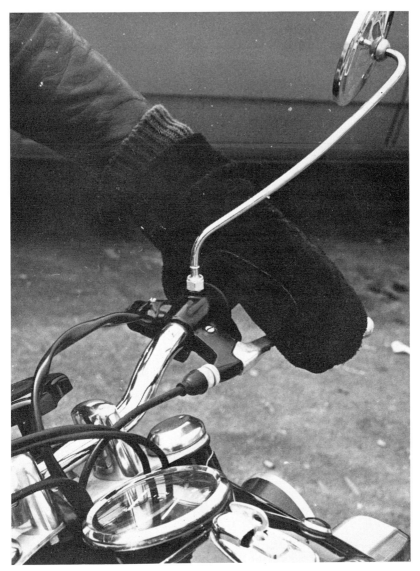

Heavy gloves or mittens are a real necessity for cold-weather riding comfort. *Ed. De Rienze Photo.*

Hands and feet are key indicators to bodily comfort. They transmit weather miseries with an emphasis all their own. Light, unlined leather gloves can be appreciated, even in summertime. Lined versions, mitts and gauntlets are the order of the day when

A well-prepared scrambles course makes a picturesque background for amateur action that draws a large field of competitors who appreciate excellent conditions under which to sharpen their riding skills. *Ed. De Rienze Photo.*

thermometers plunge. Gauntlets that attach over the handlebar grips are also worth a look. Footwear that accommodates an extra pair of socks and fends off the chill well above the ankle is the best choice for winter.

All-over relief from the blasts inspires some riders to adopt face masks of chamois leather, or knitted types worn by skiers. As good a measure as any may be simply a scarf knotted, bandit-fashion, over the nose and chin. When weather's that bad, you can be sure of one thing: There won't be any motorcycle traffic jams!

RIDE, RIDE—AND RIDE SOME MORE

More so than most motorized sports, cycling is a highly personalized skill. For instance, the bike would soon keel over without the rider's finesse in keeping it upright in motion.

The two-wheeler's extreme maneuverability on and off the road, whether the underfooting is smooth or brutal, helps account for its unique popularity. Yet it issues a sharp challenge. The rider

A modern beach scene: a wheeled twosome. *Yamaha Photo.*

must master his machine's vast potentials. As with any skill, constant practice is required. The best kind aims for improved ability to handle an infinite number of situations demanding extra know-how.

Rides should be planned to expand biking experience, in terms of weather, terrain, distance, dark and daylight, and various kinds of traffic problems. The capability of both the rider and machine should be regarded. Yet there's merit in adventuring a bit beyond the same old groove.

Maybe you won't enjoy whirring through the raindrops. But sample it for the day you may get caught in a downpour. Again, you mightn't like mushing through mud. Give it a try, and you'll at least know the basics of mud sledding.

Many motorcycle clubs have weekly mileage contests. Odometers are checked at each meeting, with a prize going to the top traveler. The main idea is to encourage everyone to roll as much as possible. All records show that the more miles of varied kinds of wheeling you can put behind your saddle, the more talented and safe rider you're likely to become.

How It "Handles" and Why

You're not an oddball if you become really fussy about the way your motorcycle, or *any* motorcycle, handles when you're calling the signals. Growing sensitivity to bike behavior, on dirt or boulevard, in fair weather or foul, is generally a sign that you're making progress. The sheer novelty of two-wheeled propulsion has worn off. No longer will you settle for any old bag of bolts, square wheels, and a rubber-band motor. No sir, you've developed some standards of your own. That iron charger had better measure up or there'll be some changes made.

At this stage, you've probably been asking yourself, "What is it about this or that machine that gives me these particular feelings when I'm on board?" Or maybe you had an experience that roused you into looking at bikes more analytically. We remember a vivid example some years ago when we first "graduated" to a 600cc highway conqueror.

Beautiful day, splendid pavement, no traffic, good, fat speed limit—so we began cranking it on: 50, 55, 60 mph and still plenty of throttle left. On up to 65, and the song of the road and the good life of riding lulled our ears. Lo, just as the needle scratched 68, we kerplunked across a little gouge in the paving—and things went haywire. The bike suddenly went into a violent cork-screwing

Getting the feel of a machine is one way to arrive at the decision of what one to purchase. *Bernhard A. Roth Photo.*

action at both ends. And all we could do was chop the throttle and cling for dear life till the bucking quit, just as suddenly, around 50 mph.

Back at the dealer's, we learned about front fork dampeners, which someone had neglected to mention. The one on our bike wasn't labeled, and we wouldn't have known what to do with it, anyway. But, thoroughly scared, we learned fast: The dampener

A picture of ultraspecialization at the height of action is seen in this shot of a Hodaka 100 and rider practicing jumps from a high berm. *Pabatco Photo.*

controls the degree of resistance in the front suspension. Ours was incorrectly set for the snappy flutter to be expected at high speed. The adjustable dampener isn't needed or installed on all machines. So it was big news to us at that time.

STUDY IN CYCLE ANATOMY

No single part or component of a motorcycle is entirely responsible for the way it acts. Rather, it's the coordinated effect of all the working bits and pieces that does the job. There's a human factor, too. The individual operator's tastes and needs surely influence his opinion of a given machine.

Rider position has a great deal to do with rider happiness and efficiency of control. The position is more or less set by the related placement, and the peculiar design of the saddle, foot pegs, handlebars, and controls. These elements must accommodate the physique of the rider. For casual cycling, few want to travel doubled up like an inchworm or sitting bolt upright. Somewhere in between is the general choice. Yet, for road racing and drags, the style is to bend over radically to cut wind resistance.

Similarly, a gung-ho dirt rider might prefer his foot pegs farther rearward than the norm. Incidentally, he might also want a narrower tank and saddle to make the often-used stand-up position even more convenient. The motorcycle is supremely adaptable among the denizens of the vehicle world. Items in your "cockpit" on board can be adjusted, moved around, and substituted to your better satisfaction.

Suspension systems, tailor-made for specialized cycling, give each model its own peculiar flavor in performance. Each system, of course, is designed to accommodate the weight, balance, dimensions, power, and other peculiarities of the machine with which it's integrated.

Dirt- and trail-bike suspension, for example, can be characterized as heavy-duty, deep-springing, to absorb the extreme, up-and-down plunging and rearing caused by wild topography. As a case in point, take the swing-arm mechanism, which suspends the rear wheels of practically all modern cycles. Terrific forces are brought to bear on the swing-arm pivot, regardless of the type of bike.

A violent twisting strain occurs when a flat-tracker is cornering for the pole position. Similar wrenching goes to work on a highway model at turnpike speed, even on a relatively mild curve. Recent efforts by designers to improve swing-arm stability have resulted in safer, more pleasant handling qualities in many diversified models.

Two suspension units vital to a rider's sensations are the front fork and the rear shock absorbers. These components have quite a bit in common, in their functions. A major difference pertains to the fork, which holds the front wheel, and therefore is also engineered for steering purposes.

Forks and shocks both have upper and lower elements. It is the

A European road racer displays championship form going through a tight bend. Perfection in manufacture of tires and suspension of modern bikes often originated from stress of competition such as this. *Avon Photo.*

interworking of these elements, aided by coiled springs and hy-draulic oil, that copes with the bumps and the ruts. Nitrogen gas is also used in some newer units. The basic aim is to cushion the downward plunge and restrict the upward recoil. In some designs, springs alone are used. In others, springs combine with the use of oil. Springs absorb the downbeat; oil under compression retards the bounce up. The latter reaction is called "dampening."

Basic front fork designs are the telescopic and the leading link. The term "telescopic" fairly well describes the way this fork works. Its elements compress and recoil in a straight-line axis. Leading link designs have an extra element consisting of a pivoting arm also attached to the front wheel axle. The objective is to permit the bike to roll over obstacles with lessened nose-dipping and lift-ing.

On modern sophisticated bikes, controls are fitted to front and rear suspension units. They allow the rider to adjust his mount to a variety of surfaces and to compensate for various passenger and luggage loads.

Steering geometry is a term often used by motorcycle techni-cians in discussing bike handling qualities. This refers to the posi-

A Pennsylvania enduro rider digs out of a two-foot-deep mudhole with his capable Yamaha 125 featuring high clearance, wide motocross handlebars, and mud-conquering knobby tires. *Bernhard A. Roth Photo.*

tioning and angling of suspension units—particularly the front fork, which is a key in steering control. Bearing in mind that the front fork-and-wheel combination acts very much like a "rudder," it's apparent that this has much to do with a cycle's responsiveness, or lack of it. Rake and trail angles of the fork are specifically designed to serve the particular model's mission in life.

Scrambler and motocross fork designs, for instance, tend toward a more vertical (to the ground) alignment. Coupled with wide handlebars, which afford better leverage, the effect is quick, whippy, sensitive steering, ideal for the mission. At the opposite end of the scale, a dragster may have radically extended suspension units, front and back, due to the dead, straight-ahead nature of its run.

Flat track stylists do a great deal of experimentation with their steering geometry in search of the perfect wedding between surging speed and knife-edge control.

Choice of wheels is still another aspect of the kind of ride each bike delivers. The key to understanding this factor is the size of wheel. For illustration, take two wheels. One is twenty-one inches;

A cross-over network of spokes is designed to supply the utmost strength in suspension for a lightweight bike. *Bernhard A. Roth Photo.*

the other is eighteen inches. (These sizes refer to diameters at the rim, which would also of course be the tire sizes.)

Naturally, the twenty-one-incher has a greater circumference. At a given bike speed, it would be turning *slower* than the eighteen-incher traveling at the same velocity over the road. The effect of relatively small wheels is often described as a "busy" ride. At highway speed, for example, you get a feeling that those little wheels are working very busily under you. You may also *hear* them more noticeably than larger wheels in motion. This is not to say that big wheels are the order of the day. Actually, motorcycle engineering takes advantage of the difference.

Larger-diameter wheels are installed at the front position in many models. And the reason is precisely as indicated above. The larger wheel will turn slower than the smaller rear one. By turning slower, the tire maintains more continuous traction with the ground or pavement. The result is better steerability.

Although this principle is most often applied to off-road machinery, it works for the boulevard jobs too. Rider slang for the big wheel/little wheel combo has found a place in cycle literature. The word is "sled."

Cycle Communicators

News of motorcycling happens fast. There are thirty-odd magazines and hundreds of writers, photographers, and broadcasters—
in the United States alone—trying to keep up with it. Every
month, newsstands sprout a fresh crop of colorful periodicals alive
with the latest biking hardware and riding action. On-the-scene re-
porters furnish readers extra ears and eyes that pick up cycle signals
around the world.

Stay tuned to one or several of these communicators. This will
insure that you won't miss a happening important to your style
of two-wheeling. Whatever your interest, you'll find at least one
periodical staff trying to package pictures and information of your
favorite brand.

You name it: racing, clubs, new models, antiques, minis, choppers, personalities, do-it-yourself mechanics, trade shows, stunts,
trail, boulevard, test ride results, new laws, safety, romance, humor,
cartoons, exploring, camping, etc. There's a steady stream for you
to dip into, according to your own thirst.

To follow the torrent of motorcycle doings closely often requires
that journalists ride hard with the pack. Most editors today have
long years in the saddle behind them. Many have diced it out in
national and international competition. A majority still throw a

Keeping close to the action for stories that "tell it like it is," Bruce Cox of *MotorCycle Weekly* tries a wet dip in a West Coast motocross. MotorCycle Weekly.

leg over a bike by personal choice, and to catch the action, close up.

Several editors volunteered friendly words for you, as a reader of *The Complete Beginner's Guide to Motorcycling*.

Charles Clayton of *Cycle News* publishes three editions that cover the West every week and the South and East every two weeks. He says, "Motorcycle riding is the nearest that one can get on earth to the mystical realm where man and the physical universe are in harmony—or else. The satisfaction of a gesture

Cycle Magazine's Cook P. Neilson (in white leathers) gives his readers "saddle-hot" editorial material. Moments after this photo was taken, Neilson recorded 164 mph in 9.08 seconds aboard an H-D 88-cubic-inch, 2-wheeled dragster. *Cycle Magazine.*

elegantly committed while riding a motorcycle is as great as the punishment for misconduct is swift. I know of no better self-teaching device for the mastery of physical laws."

Cycle Magazine is known for outspoken comparison road tests made by its own hard-riding staff of experts. Cook P. Neilson, editor, is one of the nation's top dragsters. He comments: "Motorcycling's image problem has shifted. No longer are we considered the skull-and-crossbones specialists. We are now considered the out-of-doors defilers, enemies of ecology and pernicious noise-makers. Do us all a favor: Keep your mufflers on, be polite to hikers, and try not to scare the horseback set."

Bruce Cox publishes *MotorCycle Weekly* with regular reports from former national champions including Ivan Mauger, Rod Gould, and Gary Nixon. A veteran of international class racing in Europe, himself, Cox says, "I've never found any other sport that can even come close to motorcycling for excitement and sheer good fun. However, there are certain ground rules that all bike riders should follow. Like wearing a safety helmet at all times, re-

Dave Hetzler of *Popular Cycling* started riding at age 14, raced professionally for eight years, and gears his magazine to the off-road rider looking for the greatest enjoyment. Popular Cycling.

specting other people's property, and making sure your bike is properly muffled rather than blasting out the eardrums of everybody in the neighborhood. I've found that if you follow these rules, not only do *you* enjoy bike riding, but other people let you *continue* enjoying it in the bargain."

Geared especially to off-road riding is *Popular Cycling*, for the many who find their greatest enjoyment in this form. Editor Dave Hetzler has ridden bikes for two decades, including eight years as a professional racer. His comments: "Today, motorcycling is a family sport. Mom, Dad, and the kids can thus find their common interests in the great outdoors. Getting together in this manner has got to be one of the best ways possible to bridge the so-called generation gap. Any sport that does this can't be all bad."

CYCLE PUBLICATIONS

The following list is a major sampling of periodicals available in the United States. Excellent magazines are also published abroad, and by several manufacturers who distribute them through their local dealers.

AMA NEWS, P.O. Box 231, Worthington, O. 43085.

CYCLE MAGAZINE, 1 Park Avenue, New York, N.Y. 10016.

CYCLE NEWS, 2499 Cerritos Avenue, Long Beach, Calif. 90801.

CYCLE WORLD, 1499 Monrovia Boulevard, Newport Beach, Calif. 92660.

MINIBIKE GUIDE, P.O. Box 978, North Hollywood, Calif. 91603.

MODERN CYCLE, 7805 Deering Avenue, Canoga Park, Calif. 91304.

MOTORCYCLE DEALER NEWS, 747 East Green Street, Pasadena, Calif. 91101.

MOTORCYCLE SPORT QUARTERLY, 5900 Hollywood Boulevard, Los Angeles, Calif. 90028.

MOTORCYCLE WEEKLY, 15740 Paramount Boulevard, Paramount, Calif. 90723.

MOTORCYCLIST MAGAZINE, P.O. Box 638, Sierra Madre, Calif. 91024.

POPULAR CYCLING, 131 South Barrington Place, Los Angeles, Calif. 90049.

On History Trail

The chronicle of events leading up to the shiny new motorcycle sitting on the showroom floor is getting close to a hundred years long. It is the story of many inventive geniuses in many countries adding and exchanging idea after idea to the gradual development of a vast pool of two-wheel-powered science. Although individuals and pioneer firms made major contributions, no one can be accurately credited with creating an original motorcycle unassisted by others.

A complete history of the bike should be a combined history of various components: engine; drive train; frame; seating; electrical system; suspension; wheels and tires; handlebars, and so on, and how these moved into present-day configuration. Since all these items materialized in scattered fashion, a full account of each would take volumes to describe.

There's evidence that a number of dreamers on the Continent and in England assembled contraptions vaguely resembling motorcycles in the late nineteenth century. An exhibit at the renowned cycle museum at Beaulieu in Hampshire, England, credits one Edward Butler with invention of a motorized tricycle in 1884.

However, the first *public look* at "things to come" was probably Gottlieb Daimler's machine. The wooden-frame, wooden-wheeled

For several decades, BMW's sleek side-car rigs made touring history. The newest BMWs are no longer set up for side cars due to the waning popularity among today's sports riders. Side-hack racers, too, are among the minority. *BMW Photo.*

A pre-World War II speedster was the BMW Rennesport, a road racer capable of 132 mph in the years 1938–40, with a 2-cylinder opposed engine developing 56 hp. *BMW Photo.*

vehicle powered by a 264cc air-cooled motor appeared in Germany in 1885. Recorded is a four-mile, point-to-point run made by the inventor's son at a pace approximate to walking. Two main wheels arranged in tandem were aided by a small "helper" wheel on either side. Belts and pulleys provided a two-speed drive system.

Daimler's accomplishment was preceded and made possible by development of a successful internal combustion engine eleven years previously. This was the work of Dr. Nikolaus A. Otto, also a German, in 1876. As the originator of a relatively light, compact power plant carrying its own fuel supply, Otto is often referred to as "father of the automotive age."

The earliest marketing of "production line" motorcycles is generally credited to the Hildebrand Brothers of Munich, Germany, in 1894. An initial model featured a two-cylinder Otto-related engine having a huge 1,488cc displacement. The 4-stroke design turned over at 250 rpm's developing 2½ hp. Hildebrand's tubular steel frame, bicycle-style handlebars, and low-central mounting of the engine had the general outline of a modern cycle.

By 1900, internal combustion engineers in France and Belgium led the way in producing markedly lighter, stronger, more efficient power plants. Really practical motorcycle engines, from this point, spurred the beginnings of an industry in Europe and the United States.

Gottlieb Daimler's original motorcycle. *NSU Museum.*

Bikes magnetize people, as with this Pennsylvania young couple who spend weekends at a pay-to-ride motorcycle farm, developing their off-road skills. *Bernhard A. Roth Photo.*

Indian and Harley-Davidson lines of motorcycles began manufacture in America within a year of each other, 1902–3. They were joined by nearly a hundred other makes. Among those best remembered today are Cleveland, Henderson, Pope, Pierce Arrow, Champion, Excelsior, Militor, Cyclone, and the Flying Merkel.

Over the years, Harley-Davidson survived as the only mass producer of American motorcycles. Fierce competition exerted by automobiles, and other factors, limited the growth of U.S. cycling during much of three critical decades, from 1920 to 1950. Meanwhile, the powered two-wheeler made steady progress in foreign lands. There, the need for cheap, short-range transportation was more acute.

Hampered as the American industry was, its engineers added measurably to technical developments. Beefy, reliable engines—such as four-cylinder units as early as 1912—plus automotive-type

The local cycle dealer's is a good place to find a buddy. *Ed. De Rienze Photo.*

suspension and styling, were soon devised to tame the nation's vast distances.

By 1914, Indian had discarded night lanterns and installed a forerunner of modern motorcycle electrical systems. It provided lights, ignition, and a self-starter.

Speeds to 100 mph and beyond were attained in 1930 by the Indian Scout 101, so named because it could do 101 mph. Speeds in excess of 173 mph had been reached by BMW, the still-famous German cycle firm, by 1937.

Bikedom's most famous line of heavyweights began with production of Harley-Davidson's continuing classic, the "74," in the early 1920s, along with early models of their V-Twin engines.

The current worldwide boom in motorcycling harks back to the rise of the lightweight motorcycle. No one in particular "invented" it. Its inspiration came from a number of sources.

Away back in 1912, the German NSU firm began establishing

its automotive career with a 100-pound "moped" (motor/pedal) whose 188cc plant enabled 35 mph on 1½ hp. For the next 30 years and more, many international manufacturers toyed with powered bicycles. Often these were actual pedal-pushers featuring thimble-size motors giving less than adequate propulsion. Motor scooters in the 1930s and late 1940s further whetted public expectancy for a real lightweight performer in the motorcycle mode.

In this setting, Japanese companies led by Honda unveiled the first of their featherweights to the world cycling scene, chiefly in the United States. They had tiny 50cc engines and "step through" frames. But they strongly resembled real-life motorcycles, had "grown-up" gearshift drive systems, and did a fair job of breasting the Sunday traffic. With simple gear modification, they adapted handily to trailing, camping, and other off-road recreational uses. To the American public, motorcycles had finally become the "in thing."

By the mid-1960s, lightweights in ever-refining forms had won a tenacious foothold with families throughout the world. The breed helps to account for a motorcycle population today that has increased tenfold in the past decade, in the United States alone. It did much to open the front door for mediums, heavyweights, luxury models, and other more sophisticated cycling hardware. To quote the venerable *Encyclopaedia Britannica*, "There is no doubt that the motorcycle, as 2-wheeled transport, has become firmly established in the second half of the 20th century."

Where to Ask

You may want more details on motorcycles and motorcycling than you can dig up in your own neighborhood. A carefully worded letter of inquiry to one of the following addresses may produce the advice you need.

GENERAL INFORMATION

State laws: Write to your state bureau of motor vehicles (or whatever it may be called), in care of your state capital city, for copies of motorcycle legislation that may affect you.

Federal information: For background on the federal government's activities and recommendations for motorcycle riding, safety, education, traffic control, and improved engineering, contact Motorcycle Specialist, National Highway Safety Administration, U. S. Department of Transportation, Washington, D.C. 20591.

Racing—clubs—events: Rules of competition, news of cycling clubs, listing of approved motorcycles—these and similar details may be secured by joining or writing to American Motorcycle Association, P.O. Box 231, Worthington, O. 43085.

Industry doings: Should your interest turn to what's going on inside the motorcycle business, in production figures, new plans for motorcycles, accessories, supplies and aids for the rider, there's a really good source. Most of the major firms belong to the Motorcycle Industry Council, 1001 Connecticut Avenue, N.W., Washington, D.C. 20036.

MOTORCYCLE MAKERS AND DISTRIBUTORS

These folks can help you find local dealers, parts, and services for their particular machines. They can answer the more difficult questions regarding production history, marketing plans, the availability of rider and shop manuals, and similar technical data.

Although the list is not complete, it covers the most numerous bikes marketed in the United States:

BENELLI Cosmopolitan Motors, Jacksonville and Meadowbrook Road, Hatboro, Pa. 19040.

BMW   Butler & Smith, Inc., Walnut Street and Hudson Avenue, Norwood, N.J. 07648.

BRIDGESTONE Rockford Motors, 191 Harrison Avenue, Rockford, Ill. 61100.

BSA and TRIUMPH Birmingham Small Arms Company, Inc., P.O. Box 275, Duarte, Calif. 91010.

BULTACO Cemoto East Importing Company, Inc., Box 1065, 2040 Maxon Road, Schenectady, N.Y. 12301.

GREEVES Nick Nicholson Motors, 11629 Van Owen, North Hollywood, Calif. 91600.

HARLEY-DAVIDSON Harley-Davidson Motor Company, P.O. Box 653, Milwaukee, Wis. 53201.

HODAKA Pacific Basin Trading Company, Box 327, Athena, Ore. 97813.

HONDA American Honda Motor Company, Inc., 100 West Alondra Boulevard, Gardena, Calif. 92047.

HUSQVARNA Husqvarna of Sweden, Inc., 151 New World Way, South Plainfield, N.J. 07080.

JAWA American Jawa Ltd., 185 Express Street, Plainview, L.I., N.Y. 91316.

KAWASAKI Kawasaki Motors Corporation, 1062 McGaw Avenue, Santa Ana, Calif. 92705.

MONTESA Montesa Motors, 3657 Beverly Boulevard, Los Angeles, Calif. 90004.

NORTON Berliner Motor Corporation, Railroad Street and Plant Road, Hasbrouck Heights, N.J. 07604.

OSSA Yankee Motor Corporation, P.O. Box 36, Schenectady, N.Y. 12300.

STEEN Steen's Inc., 1635 West Valley Boulevard, Alhambra, Calif. 91800.

SUZUKI U. S. Suzuki Motor Corporation, 13767 Freeway Drive, Santa Fe Springs, Calif. 90670.

YAMAHA Yamaha International Corporation, 6600 Orange Thorpe, Buena Park, Calif. 90620.

Index

BERNHARD A. ROTH, former editor of a leading sportsmen's magazine, has been a freelance writer for many years, concentrating on travel, outdoor recreation, and conservation. He is chief public information officer serving the Northeast and Caribbean areas for the United States Department of Agriculture Soil Conservation Service. A veteran of motorcycling on three continents, he is also a sailplane pilot and a member of the Outdoor Writers of America.

He is married with three children and lives in a suburb of Philadelphia, Pennsylvania. Mr. Roth writes a weekly column of motorcycling news.

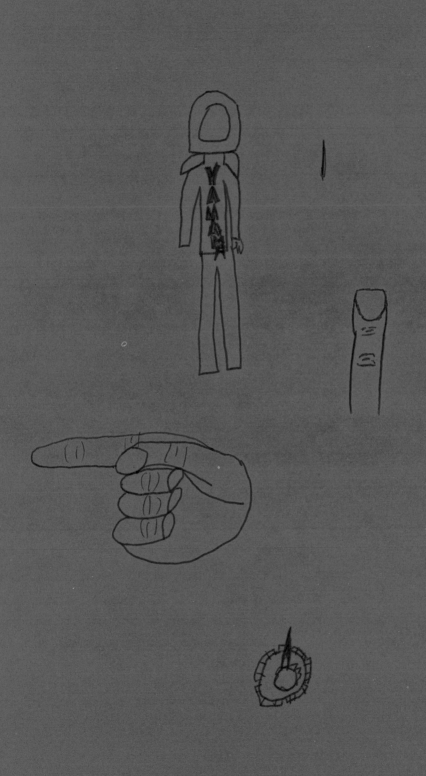